Eating well for under-5s in child care

Practical and nutritional guidelines

REPORT OF AN EXPERT WORKING GROUP

THE CAROLINE WALKER TRUST

Acknowledgements

The Caroline Walker Trust would like to thank the Members of the Expert Working Group for their time and expertise in compiling this report.

© The Caroline Walker Trust, 1998

ISBN 1 897820 07 0

Published by:

The Caroline Walker Trust
P O Box 61
St Austell
PL26 6YL
Tel: 01726 844107

Registered charity number: 328580

Edited and produced by Wordworks, London W4 2HY.
Design by Information Design Workshop.
Cover illustration based on a drawing by Matthew, aged 4.

Further copies of this report are available from: Eating Well for Under-5s in Child Care, PO Box 5, Manchester M60 3GE. Credit card orders on: 0870-608 0213. Price £12.95 including postage and packing.

Other publications by The Caroline Walker Trust and available from the same PO Box address:

Nutritional Guidelines for School Meals

Eating Well for Older People

CORA Menu Planner: Eating Well for Older People
A computer program to help plan menus for older people, published by The Caroline Walker Trust and DGAA. Tel: 0171-396 6745.

Foreword

The Caroline Walker Trust is dedicated to the improvement of public health through good food. Established in 1988 to continue the work of the distinguished nutritionist, writer and campaigner Caroline Walker, the Trust is a charity which undertakes specific projects as a result of grants and donations. A major part of our work is to produce expert reports which establish nutritional guidelines for vulnerable groups. *Eating Well for Under-5s in Child Care* is our third expert report and we hope it will have the same stimulating and practical impact as the previous two - *Nutritional Guidelines for School Meals* and *Eating Well for Older People*.

The impetus for this expert report came from a recognition that increasing numbers of under-5s are spending long periods of time in child care outside their own homes - in local authority or private nurseries, with childminders, or in other forms of child care. This has obvious implications for the nutritional status of these children as a large proportion of their meals and snacks are now consumed outside the home. The proposal to produce this report was warmly welcomed by those working in the field of child care.

There is evidence that the diets of under-5s in the UK are too low in vitamins A and C, too low in iron and zinc and, for some groups of children, too low in vitamin D. Children's diets also contain too much of the type of sugars that most contribute to tooth damage. However, until the publication of this report there were no nutritional guidelines for food prepared for children in child care settings.

Healthy eating and physical activity are vital for proper growth and development in childhood. Those who provide child care are in a unique position to have a positive influence not only on the nutritional intake of these children but also on the knowledge and attitudes they have towards food and a healthy lifestyle.

We have been very encouraged and impressed by the support and enthusiasm of those who provide child care. They clearly recognise the important role they can play in encouraging healthy development through good food for the children in their care. We hope that this report will make a useful contribution to raising awareness of the importance of healthy, balanced diets for the under-5s and that the nutritional guidelines are accepted as standards for children in child care.

We would particularly like to thank the Members of the Expert Working Group who so generously gave their time and expertise, and Dr Helen Crawley, Rosie Leyden and Sarah Ivatts who between them efficiently and effectively provided the research and writing, editing and design, and the administrative back-up for this report. We also thank the Nutrition Section of the Department of Health for providing the financial support which enabled us to produce the report. We would like to make particular mention of Dr Petra Clarke who retires from the Department of Health as this report goes to press and whose expertise and support have been invaluable.

We hope that carers of children under 5 will enjoy reading the report and that it will be a useful contribution to re-establishing good food as the basis of good health.

Maggie Sanderson
Chair of The Caroline Walker Trust
and
Anne Dillon Roberts
Trustee of The Caroline Walker Trust and Chair of the Expert Group

Contents

Chapter 1

Summary and recommendations

This report deals with children up to their fifth birthday. The term 'infants' applies to children up to 12 months. The term 'under-5s' applies to children from 12 months to their fifth birthday. The term 'carers' applies to staff working in child care and early years settings including local authority and private nurseries, and childminders.

'A table full of food, with legs for the table so it won't fall over.'
Michael, aged 4

Summary

Healthy eating and physical activity are essential for proper growth and development in childhood. To help children develop patterns of healthy eating from an early age, it is important that the food and eating patterns to which they are exposed - both at home and outside the home - are those which promote positive attitudes to good nutrition.

Growing children need plenty of energy (calories) and nutrients to ensure they grow and develop well. A good appetite will usually make sure they get enough energy from the food they eat. However, there is evidence[1] that:

- the diets of children under 5 in Britain are:
  - too low in vitamin A
  - too low in vitamin C
  - too low in iron
  - too low in zinc and
  - for some groups of children, too low in vitamin D
- their diets contain too much of the type of sugars that most contribute to tooth damage.

Intakes of meat, fish, vegetables and fruit are generally low. An increase in the intakes of these foods would help to ensure that children have the right amounts of vitamins and minerals for healthy growth and development.

Eating is an important part of everyone's life. Encouraging children to eat healthily does not mean denying them food they enjoy. Healthy eating is about getting a varied, balanced diet and enjoying lots of different foods.

Under-5s in child care

The number of children under the age of 5 who spend some time being cared for outside the family home has risen dramatically in recent years. It is estimated that, of a total population of about 3,150,000 under-5s in England, 365,000 (12%) are looked after by childminders, 172,000 (6%) are cared for in registered private nurseries, and 20,200 (less than 1%) in local authority day nurseries.[2] In addition, many other children are looked after by privately arranged nannies, au pairs or mother's helps.

Day care providers supply an increasing proportion of the total food eaten by children in their care. Although many aspects of child care outside the home are regulated or monitored, the nutritional quality of food is not, and there are currently no guidelines to enable this process.

The way forward

The Caroline Walker Trust therefore identified a need for clear, practical guidelines which encourage healthy eating among the under-5s in child care. With the support of the Department of Health, the Trust brought together an Expert Working Group to produce nutritional guidelines. These guidelines indicate the proportion of energy and nutrients that should be provided by food offered during child care. Specific nutritional guidelines are given for:

- children under 5 in child care for a full day
- children in half-day care including lunch, and
- children in half-day care including tea.

The guidelines are shown and explained in chapter 6. Information on nutrition – which readers may find helpful in interpreting the guidelines – is given in chapter 3.

Chapter 6 also gives some sample menus which meet the guidelines. These will give readers an idea of how the nutritional guidelines can be translated into practice.

The report also gives recommendations about food choice and food service and about the importance of physical activity.

The provision of a well balanced diet to infants and under-5s is crucial to children's health and wellbeing. The Expert Working Group recommends that the nutritional guidelines and other recommendations contained in this report should become standards for child care. It is also suggested that local authorities organise appropriate nutritional training for carers, and that Government will support this work.

Recommendations

The following recommendations apply to children aged between 1 and 5 years, unless otherwise specified. Separate recommendations for infants up to the age of 12 months are given on page 14.

Nutritional guidelines

1 Nutritional guidelines for food for under-5s in child care are given on pages 57 and 58 of this report. These guidelines should become standards for child care.

2 Government departments should include reference to these nutritional guidelines in guidance and legislation on child care.

3 Government and local authorities should include nutrition and nutritional guidelines in development plans for children under 5 in child care, and in plans for early years services and education.

4 Local authorities should adopt the nutritional guidelines and use them as standards in the nurseries and child care settings which they contract, register, monitor and inspect.

5 Local authorities should ensure that they either have, or have access to, appropriately skilled and trained staff to enable them to monitor nutritional standards in child care settings.

6 Local authorities should provide the necessary training and information to enable individual carers to use the nutritional guidelines effectively.

7 Registration and inspection officers should monitor the nutritional standards of the food served in the child care and other early years settings they visit. Inspectors' reports should include comments on food and nutrition. Appropriate expert advice and help should be offered to any child care or other early years setting which does not meet the guidelines.

8 Registration and inspection officers should look for management commitment to nutritional training of a key person in each child care or other early years setting.

9 Child care and other early years settings should be required, as part of the registration process, to demonstrate that they are committed to providing food which meets these guidelines.

10 Nursery owners, managers, caterers, childminders and others responsible for early years services should seek appropriate information and training on how to meet the nutritional guidelines.

11 NVQs, SVQs and the Certificate in Childcare and Education (CCE) are important training opportunities for carers and other early years staff. The information in this report should become an integral part of those qualifications within the relevant units. Other qualifications for those caring for under-5s should contain an appropriate section on nutrition and healthy eating.

12 The European Commission should take account of the nutritional guidelines in this report when looking at European-wide nutritional standards for under-5s within the Community.

Eating for health

13 Children should be encouraged to eat a varied diet. They should eat foods from each of the four main food groups every day. The four main food groups are:

- bread, other cereals and potatoes
- fruit and vegetables
- milk and dairy foods, and
- meat, fish and alternatives such as pulses (peas, beans and lentils), and soya.

A varied diet is associated with better health as it is more likely to contain all the nutrients the body needs.

14 Fruit and vegetables are particularly important for good health. Under-5s should be encouraged to eat five child-sized portions of fruit and vegetables a day: for example, half an apple; two portions of vegetables (such as peas, carrots or tomatoes); a glass of fruit juice (diluted, and preferably served with a meal); and a small banana or a dried fruit snack (eg raisins).

15 Vitamin C is important in maintaining good health and has a role in helping the body to absorb iron if both nutrients are present in the same meal. Under-5s should be encouraged to eat foods containing vitamin C - for example most fruit and fruit juices, potatoes, broccoli and other green vegetables, tomatoes and peppers. Eating five portions of fruit and vegetables a day (see recommendation 14) will ensure an adequate vitamin C intake.

16 It is recommended that children up to the age of 5 years should receive vitamin drops containing vitamins A, C and D. This is the responsibility of the parents or guardians but carers could provide information about where to find out more about them. See recommendation 46.

17 The iron intake of children under 5 is lower than currently recommended and there is evidence to suggest that low iron status is common in this age group. Under-5s should therefore eat a diet that is high in iron-rich food such as meat, poultry and fish, as well as fruits and vegetables. (Meat and meat dishes are also a good source of zinc.) Children who do not eat meat should have a varied diet containing foods such as cereals, pulses (peas, beans and lentils), vegetables and fruits.

18 The intakes of the type of sugars in the diet which most contribute to tooth decay are higher than recommended among the under-5s. If children have sugary foods, these should be given with meals rather than as snacks between meals. Children do not need sugary foods such as sweets, chocolate, soft drinks or honey for energy. Starchy foods - such as potatoes, bread, rice, pasta and yam - are better sources of energy as these foods contain other important nutrients too.

19 It is important that the under-5s get enough energy (calories) for growth and development. While adults and children aged over 5 are encouraged to eat a diet that is high in starchy foods and low in fat, younger children on this sort of diet may not have the appetite to eat enough food to provide all the nutrients they need. Carers should therefore be sensitive to the needs of children who are fussy eaters or small eaters and ensure that these children are offered food that they will accept.

Drinks for 1 to 5 year olds

20 Children should be encouraged to drink water if they are thirsty. Water quenches thirst, does not spoil the appetite, and does not damage teeth.

21 Milk is a good drink for 1 to 5 year olds. Whole cow's milk is suitable as a main drink for most children from 12 months of age. Semi-skimmed milk can be introduced gradually after the age of 2 years, provided that the child is a good eater and has a varied diet. Skimmed milk is not suitable as the main drink for children under 5 years of age.

22 Diluted fruit juice is a useful source of vitamin C. Children should be encouraged to have a glass of diluted fruit juice with their main meal or with breakfast as this may also help the body to absorb iron.

23 Children should be discouraged from having fizzy drinks and squashes (including fruit squashes), both diet and non-diet, as these can erode the tooth enamel and contribute to tooth decay. Also, they provide little in the way of nutrients, and children who drink them frequently may have less appetite to eat well at mealtimes.

24 If children are given soft drinks (such as squashes) containing the intense sweetener saccharin, these should be diluted more than they would be for an adult or older child - for example, 1 part squash to at least 8 parts water.

25 Children who bring their own drinks to child care should be encouraged to bring a plastic flask or a lidded plastic cup containing an appropriately diluted drink. Many ready-to-drink cartons of squashes, fruit drinks and fruit juices have a high sugar content and cannot be diluted if they are drunk straight from the pack.

26 Tea and coffee are not suitable drinks for under-5s as they contain tannic acid which interferes with iron absorption.

Dental health

27 If children are having sugary foods and drinks, these should be given with meals rather than between meals. This is because children's first teeth are prone to decay if they are frequently in contact with sugars. It is important to reduce both the frequency and the total amount of sugar and sugary foods that children eat.

28 To help the healthy development of teeth, children should not be given sweet drinks (such as fruit juice, squashes and other soft drinks) in a bottle or dinky feeder. A cup or beaker should be used if these drinks are given with meals.

29 If a child uses a dummy or comforter, it should never be dipped into sugar or sugary drinks, as this can contribute to tooth decay.

30 Some soft drinks which claim to have 'no added sugar' still contain sugars which are harmful to the teeth. Diet drinks, both fizzy and still, can also be harmful to the teeth. This is because they may be acidic and erode the dental enamel, especially if sipped frequently. The use of these drinks should be avoided or limited.

These recommendations apply to children aged between 1 and 5 years, unless otherwise specified. Separate recommendations for infants up to the age of 12 months are given on page 14.

Physical activity and outdoor play

31 Children should be encouraged to be physically active and carers should timetable periods of activity into the children's daily routine throughout the year. Physical activity helps to ensure that children eat enough food and get all the nutrients they need. It also builds up muscle strength and overall fitness, develops physical skills such as balance and coordination, and provides a release for children's energy. Children who are physically active when they are young are more likely to maintain a healthy active lifestyle as they get older. This is important as an active lifestyle reduces the risk of ill health in adulthood.

32 It is essential that there is outdoor space where children can play, or access to an outside area such as a garden, park or other safe open space. Exposure to summer sunlight in outdoor play helps children to maintain their vitamin D status. However, child care settings should have a 'sun policy', with guidelines on how long children can remain outdoors in strong sunshine, and on the use of protective clothing such as sunhats, and a sun screen. All under-5s should be appropriately supervised at all times while outdoors.

33 Children in child care should have access to toys for active play - for example balls, hoops and skipping ropes.

Organisation of mealtimes and snacks

Timing of meals and snacks

34 Breakfast is a particularly important meal and fortified breakfast cereals can make an important contribution to daily vitamin and mineral intakes. Parents and guardians should work together with carers to ensure that children have breakfast, either at home or in child care.

35 Children need to eat regularly and it is recommended that children are offered something to eat at least every three hours.

36 Children need nutritious snacks

'Girl skipping and boy on skateboard in the park.' Ella, aged 4

'A table set for dinner with apples, drinks, spaghetti, doughnuts and an orange.'

Hannah, aged 4

between meals. The best snacks are those which are low in added sugar. A variety of snacks should be offered including fruit, vegetables and any type of bread such as sandwiches, teacakes or fruit buns.

Creating the right atmosphere and encouraging social skills

37 Meals can be times of pleasant social sharing. It is good practice for carers to sit with children during meals and snacks. It is important that what the carer eats and drinks provides a good role model for healthy eating.

38 Mealtimes offer an opportunity to extend children's social and language skills. Children can learn from the carer about table manners, and can practise their speaking and listening skills. To encourage this, distractions such as television are best avoided during mealtimes.

39 Children aged 2-5 years should be allowed to serve themselves during meals as this may encourage them to try different kinds of foods. Finger foods of all kinds, particularly fruit and vegetables, will encourage children under 2 years of age to feed themselves and try new foods. Child-sized utensils, crockery, tables and chairs may also make it easier for children to serve themselves and learn to eat independently.

40 Children should be allowed to make their own food choices. If a child refuses a food or meal, the carer should gently encourage them to eat, but children should never be forced to eat. To minimise food refusal, it is important to ensure that a variety of foods are offered.

41 Some children may eat slowly. It is important to ensure that all children have enough time to eat.

Involving parents and guardians

42 A real partnership between parents or guardians and carers should be fostered. This could include:
• making menus available to parents
• giving parents adequate notice of any changes to meals, food choice or any other aspect of food provision, and allowing them to comment on and discuss the changes before they are introduced.

43 Carers should give parents or guardians clear information each day about what food has been eaten and if their child has eaten well. Even older children may not be accurate in reporting what they have eaten.

44 Carers should ask parents or guardians about any special dietary requirements their child has before the child starts attending the child care setting. Parents of children who are on special diets (for example a gluten-free diet), or who have food intolerances, are responsible for providing the carer with information about the food choices available to their child.

45 Carers should seek advice from parents and guardians if they are serving food which the carers themselves are not familiar with. Such food should not only contain the right ingredients but should look and taste right too.

These recommendations apply to children aged between 1 and 5 years, unless otherwise specified. Separate recommendations for infants up to the age of 12 months are given on page 14.

46 Carers may wish to remind parents of the importance of giving vitamin drops to under-5s. Vitamin drops containing vitamins A, C and D are available free to families receiving Income Support or income-based Jobseeker's Allowance. Parents can get more information from their Health Visitor or GP.

Food hygiene and safety issues

47 Carers should always wash their hands with soap and water before preparing food or helping children to eat, and after changing nappies and toileting children. If carers use a handkerchief while preparing food, they should wash their hands before continuing.

48 Children's hands should always be washed with soap and water before meals and snacks, and after going to the toilet.

49 Carers need to be aware of the requirements of the Food Safety Act. Some carers may need to complete a Food Hygiene Certificate course. Further information on this can be obtained from the local authority's environmental health department, or from its registration and inspection unit.

50 Carers also need to be aware of food safety issues such as storage of food and leftover food, and thorough cooking or heating of foods. Several useful publications are available from the Ministry of Agriculture, Fisheries and Food (see Appendix 5). Carers should obtain and follow the advice in these. Some of the main points for carers are given in chapter 5.

51 Children under 5 should never be left alone while they are eating, in case they choke.

See also 'Food hygiene and safety issues for infants' on page 15.

Learning through food

52 Food can be used in a variety of educational ways, for example to teach children about food sources, nutrition, health, the seasons, growing cycles and other people's ways of life. Learning how to choose and enjoy many different nutritious foods in early childhood can provide the foundation for a lifetime of wise food choices.

53 Carers should involve children in preparing food and laying and clearing tables.

54 Holidays, festivals and religious occasions provide a valuable opportunity for children to learn about different cultures and special events and the variety of foods associated with these events.

Equal opportunities

55 All children, and their parents or guardians, should be respected as individuals, and their food preferences and religious requirements should be accommodated.

56 When planning food provision and menus, carers need to consider children who have special needs. Some children may have particular dietary requirements or may need specific help with eating, both of which are outside the scope of this report. Parents or guardians and carers may find it useful to contact support groups associated with the child's particular disability or need.

57 Carers should positively encourage both boys and girls to participate in all activities, including food-related activities such as cooking.

58 All that children bring with them to their place of child care - their race, gender, family background, language, culture and religion - should be valued in order for children to feel accepted and accepting of themselves. It is therefore important to value the contributions which different cultures and nationalities make to the variety of foods eaten in the UK today.

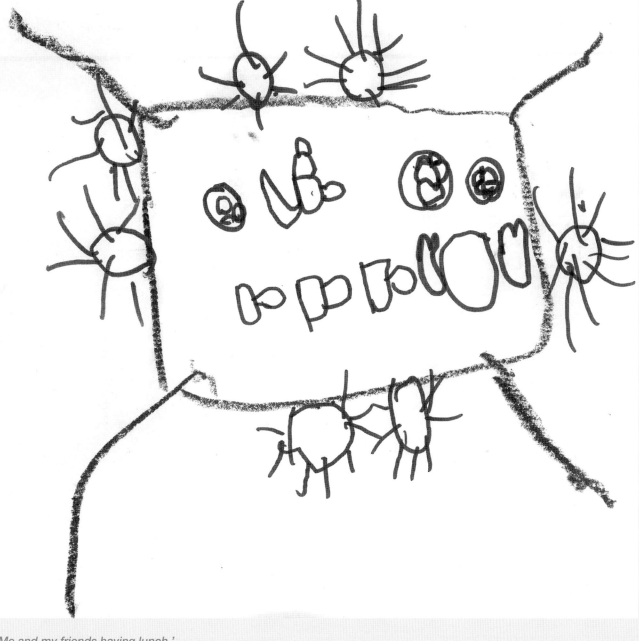

'Me and my friends having lunch.'
Ella, aged 4

Infants (children under 12 months)

The Expert Working Group recognises that many infants under the age of 12 months enter child care. Guidelines on infant nutrition are given in chapter 4 and are summarised here.

Drinks

1 Breast milk is the best food for infants. Carers should support breastfeeding mothers and encourage them to continue providing breast milk. Mothers who are breastfeeding and who may wish to feed their baby in the child care setting should have warm, private facilities made available to them.

2 If expressed breast milk is not provided, infants should be given an appropriate infant formula.

3 Babies who are bottle fed should be held and have warm physical contact with an attentive adult while being fed. Babies should be fed by the same person at each feed.

4 Babies should never be left propped up with bottles as this is both dangerous and inappropriate to babies' emotional needs.

5 From 6 months of age, infants should be introduced to drinking from a cup or beaker, and from the age of 12 months, they should be discouraged from drinking from a bottle.

6 Cow's milk is not suitable as a main drink for infants under 12 months. However, whole cow's milk can be used as an ingredient in weaning foods - for example to moisten mashed potato.

7 If drinks other than milk or water are given - for example baby juices or baby drinks - these should be diluted with at least 8 parts water and should be confined to mealtimes. Because of the risk to dental health, children over 6 months should not be given these drinks in a feeding bottle. Water given to children under 6 months, either directly or in a diluted drink, should be boiled and cooled first.

8 Adult-type soft drinks or 'diet' drinks, tea and coffee are not recommended for infants.

See also 'Dental health' on page 9.

Weaning (from 4-6 months)

9 Foods containing gluten (such as bread, pasta or chapatis) should not be given to infants under 6 months.

10 Salt should not be added to foods for infants.

11 Naturally sweet fruits (such as apples or bananas) can be used to sweeten foods rather than adding sugar.

12 Artificial sweeteners should not be added to foods for infants.

13 Soft cooked meat, fish and pulses (for example peas, beans and lentils) are suitable foods to include in the diet from 4-6 months.

14 It is important to offer a variety of flavours and soft textures. Between 6 and 12 months, food should be given which allows the infant to learn to chew and accept a wide variety of food textures.

15 If using commercial weaning foods, follow the manufacturer's instructions carefully.

16 Eggs given to babies or toddlers should be cooked until both the yolk and the white are solid.

17 Because children in the first year of life are following individual feeding and sleeping patterns, it is recommended that these are not disrupted but wherever possible integrated into the carer's timetable for the day.

18 It is recommended that children up to the age of 5 years should receive vitamin drops containing vitamins A, C and D. This is the responsibility of the parents or guardians but carers could provide information about where to find out more about them. See recommendation 46 on page 12.

Food hygiene and safety issues for infants

19 Expressed breast milk provided for babies in child care should be clearly labelled with the child's name and the date, stored in a refrigerator and only used for that child. Any expressed milk left over at the end of the day should be returned to the parent or guardian.

20 Parents of children who take infant formula should be encouraged to prepare their child's own feeds. Feeds should be labelled with the child's name and the time and day the feed was made, and should be stored in a refrigerator. Any infant formula left over at the end of the day should be returned to the parent or guardian.

21 If the carer is making up infant formula, it is preferable if it can be made in a separate milk preparation area.

22 Carers should take particular care if milk is heated in bottles. Ideally a bottle warmer should be used. If the bottle is heated by standing it in hot water, this should be done in an area which children do not have access to. A microwave should not be used to heat milk as the milk can become very hot even though the container still feels only warm.

23 Bottles and teats for infants under 6 months of age should be thoroughly cleaned and sterilised. The teats of bottles for older infants should be thoroughly cleaned.

24 If dummies or comforters are used they should be thoroughly cleaned and sterilised for infants under 6 months, and thoroughly cleaned for older infants. These recommendations also apply to dummies or comforters which are dropped.

25 If the carer is serving food from a can or jar and the child is unlikely to eat all the contents, a portion should be spooned into a separate dish or container before serving it to the child. Any unused portions should be stored according to the manufacturer's instructions. (If there are no instructions, the safest option is to throw the unused portion away.) If food is served straight from the jar and the child does not finish it, the remainder should be thrown away.

26 Any uneaten food which parents have brought in should be returned to them at the end of the day.

See also 'Food hygiene and safety issues' on page 12.

'My favourite lunch in space.'
Mustafa, aged 4½

Chapter 2

Why nutritional guidelines are needed

'I like fish fingers, sausages and chips.'

Howard, aged 3 1/2

Healthy eating and physical activity are essential for growth and development in childhood. To help children develop healthy eating patterns from an early age, it is important that the food and eating patterns to which they are exposed - both at home and outside the home - are those which promote positive attitudes to good nutrition.

The diet of under-5s in Britain

Growing children need plenty of energy and other nutrients to ensure they grow and develop normally. A good appetite will usually make sure they get enough energy from the food they eat, but there is evidence that children under 5 in Britain are consuming diets higher in the type of sugar that damages teeth than is currently recommended.[1] In addition, the intakes of some vitamins and minerals have been found to be lower than the levels which are likely to fulfil the nutrient needs of most children. Intakes of vitamin A, vitamin C, iron and zinc in particular have been found to be low among a considerable proportion of children under 5.[1] Intakes of meat, fish, vegetables and fruit are generally low. Increasing intakes of these foods would help to ensure that children have the right amounts of vitamins and minerals for adequate growth and development.

Under-5s in child care

The number of children under the age of 5 spending some time being cared for outside the family home has risen substantially as an increasing number of mothers of young children return to the workforce.

There are a number of options for parents and guardians who require child care for their children, both formal and informal. It is estimated that, of a total population of about 3,150,000 under-5s in England, 365,000 (12%) are looked after by childminders, 172,000 (6%) are cared for in registered private nurseries, and 20,200 (less than 1%) in local authority day nurseries.[2] (See *Child care in England, 1997*, below.) These figures do not include children who are looked after by privately arranged nannies, au pairs or mother's helps. A recent estimate from a survey of children aged 6-18 months suggests that, of those children cared for by someone other than their parents for at least two hours a week, 28% were cared for by childminders, 12% by nurseries, and 8% by nannies.[3]

The type of child care used by parents or guardians of the under-5s depends on what is available and what they can afford, and may change as the child gets older. Parents may choose nursery schools or pre-school playgroups to socialise and stimulate their children before schooling begins, rather than primarily as a form of child care. In many cases there is a combination of these forms of care: for example, a childminder may look after a child during parental working hours when the child is not at nursery school or playgroup.

The number of workplace nurseries remains small. Only 1 in 250 pre-school children in child care has access to employer-sponsored nursery places, and half of these places are in hospitals and universities.[5] In some areas there are also 'community nurseries' which are registered charities part-funded by the local authorities and run mainly by parents.

A working parent who pays for child care for pre-school children commits an average of 30% of their take-home pay to the cost of child care.[5]

Food provision in child care

Although many aspects of child care outside the home are regulated or monitored, the provision of food is not, and there are no guidelines to enable this process. Although parents or guardians have the main responsibility for providing adequate and appropriate food for their children, day care providers supply an increasing proportion of the total food eaten by children in their care.

There is very little information available about the provision of food for children under 5 in child care. There are no published, large-scale studies which compare the diets of children in the UK attending child care facilities with the diets of those remaining in the family home. Nor are there any published studies which determine the proportion of nutrients children receive from the food they have while in child care. There is a particular lack of information about food provided by childminders, even though this group of carers represents the largest form of paid child care in the UK.

A national survey of the eating habits of children aged $1^{1}/_{2}$ - $4^{1}/_{2}$ years (including children looked after at home and those cared for in child care settings) found that one-fifth of the average energy (calorie) intake of children in that age group came from foods eaten outside the home.[1] (Measuring average energy intake is one way of calculating the proportions of food eaten in different places or settings.) The 2.5% of children in this age group who had the highest average energy intake from foods eaten outside the home, consumed on average 75% of their food energy outside the home. This suggests that some children may have consumed the majority of their food on weekdays while in some form of child care.

Child care in England, 1997

Childminders

Registered childminders	98,500
Number of places	**365,000**

Day nurseries

Local authority day nurseries	530
Places in local authority day nurseries	**20,200**
Registered private nurseries	5,500
Places in registered private nurseries	**172,000**

Playgroups

Number of playgroups	15,800
Number of places in playgroups	**383,700**

Source: See reference 2.

Nursery schools, infant schools and independent schools (3 and 4 year olds) in England*

Full-time	**37,920**
Part-time	**380,420**

* These figures are for 1996.
Source: See reference 4.

Small-scale local surveys of food provision in child care settings suggest that there is a wide variation in the quality and quantity of food provision. Although these studies cannot be assumed to be representative of nurseries overall, they are interesting case studies in the absence of other information. One such study, in a private registered nursery in the London borough of Hounslow, examined the nutritional content of the three meals a day eaten by 16 children on a full-time care programme.[6] These children consumed a high quantity of sugars, mainly from drinks of squash. Milk as a drink was not on offer to children every day in this nursery. The children's intakes of iron, calcium, zinc and vitamin C were low in proportion to their intakes of energy and protein. Vegetarian children at the nursery were given the same main meal as non-vegetarian children but with the meat removed: for example chicken chow mein with the chicken picked out before serving.

Another small study compared the midday meals provided to children in three different types of nursery: a local authority nursery, a private registered nursery and a community nursery, all within an inner London borough.[7] Vegetables and fruit were particularly lacking in the meals provided in the private day nursery. Protein intakes were generally high but the main meals were low in iron, calcium, vitamin A, vitamin C and folate.

Those who provide child care for the under-5s are in a unique position to have a positive influence not only on the nutritional intake of those children but also on the knowledge and attitudes they have towards food and a healthy lifestyle. A successful approach to food intake requires that those providing child care have a commitment to good practice as well as an appropriate nutrition policy.

Those who provide child care for the under-5s are in a unique position to have a positive influence not only on the nutritional intake of those children but also on the knowledge and attitudes they have towards food and a healthy lifestyle.

Aims of this report

It was against this background that The Caroline Walker Trust identified a need for clear, practical and nutritional guidelines for food provided for under-5s in child care. With the financial support of the Department of Health, the Trust brought together an Expert Working Group to produce this report. A list of Members of the Group is given on page 3.

The aims of this report are:

- To provide clear, referenced background information about the relationship between good nutrition and health and development among infants and children under 5.

- To provide practical guidelines to enable local authorities, caterers, nursery owners and managers, childminders, cooks/chefs and others responsible for providing food for infants and under-5s in child care and other early years settings, to develop suitable menus which achieve a good nutritional balance and variety.

- To act as a resource document for those working for better standards of nutrition for infants and under-5s in child care and other early years settings.

This report deals with children up to their fifth birthday. In the report, the term 'infants' applies to children up to 12 months. The term 'under-5s' applies to children from 12 months to their fifth birthday. The term 'carers' applies to staff working in child care and other early years settings including local authority and private nurseries, and childminders.

Who the report is for

The four main audiences for the report are:

- Local authority departments who contract, register, monitor and inspect nurseries, childminders and other child care and early years settings

- Owners, managers, catering staff, local authority staff, childminders and other carers in environments providing child care for infants and under-5s

- Parents and guardians of infants and children under 5 who will be using child care facilities outside their own homes

- MPs, MEPs (Members of the European Parliament), civil servants, writers and journalists who may wish to know more about aspects of the nutritional needs of infants and under-5s in child care.

The provision of food to infants and under-5s is crucial to children's health and wellbeing. The Expert Working Group hopes that the nutritional guidelines contained in this report become accepted standards and recommends that all those involved in the care of infants and under-5s should adopt the nutritional guidelines and put the recommendations into practice.

Chapter 3

Nutrition and 1 to 5 year olds

'A packet of spaghetti, a bag of pears, a carrot and a bag of plums.'

Holly, aged 4

The following information applies to children aged between 12 months and 5 years, unless otherwise specified. Information on infants up to the age of 12 months is given in chapter 4.

This chapter provides the basic nutrition information needed to use the nutritional guidelines for under-5s in child care given in this report. It looks at energy (calories), protein, fat, carbohydrates, fibre and some of the important vitamins and minerals needed by the under 5s. It outlines why they are needed, how much children need, and whether they are getting enough or too much based on current scientific evidence.

Nutritional guidelines are expressed in terms of the amounts of individual nutrients needed for good health. Most foods contain a number of different nutrients so it is the *balance* of different foods within a person's eating pattern which determines whether the recommendations for 'healthy eating' are met, rather than whether a person is eating particular foods. It is important that children are given varied diets if they are to obtain all the nutrients their bodies need. How children can achieve the balance of nutrients they need from the food they eat is considered in chapter 5.

Energy (calories)

Why children need energy

Children need a certain amount of energy (calories) to enable them to function and be active. The body gets energy from fat, carbohydrate and protein (and in adults from alcohol), but most energy needs are met by fat and carbohydrate.

Children also need energy (calories) for growth and development. This is particularly important in children up to the age of 5 years as this is a time of rapid growth in muscles and bone tissues and in the development of the brain.

Energy is measured in kilocalories (kcals), which is a metric term for calories. It can also be expressed in kiloJoules (kJ). 1kcal equals approximately 4.2 kJ.

The importance of physical activity in the under 5s

The energy we need every day is determined both by a basic level of requirement to keep our bodies functioning (called the Basal Metabolic Rate or BMR) and by the amount of physical activity that we do (for example moving around, walking, or exercising). People who are inactive have lower energy needs and will eat less food to maintain their body weight. It becomes much harder to get all the nutrients needed for good health if less food is eaten.

Physical activity is essential for optimal growth and development in children. It is generally agreed that children now are less active than those in previous generations. This has been caused by a number of factors including, for example, the time spent watching television.[3] A number of studies have reported falling activity levels among young children due to a more sedentary lifestyle.[4, 5] Restrictions on children being able to walk to school or play freely outside, for safety reasons, also contribute to this.[6]

It is suggested that overweight is as much a problem of too little activity as of overeating.[7] Obesity in children is difficult to treat as care must be taken to maintain growth and development. Overweight children should be encouraged to increase their activity.[8]

It is also important that children play outside, particularly in the summer months, to ensure they get exposure to summer sunlight for the production of vitamin D. However, they should maintain adequate cover-up to prevent sunburn.

How much energy do children need? Where do they get their energy (calories) from?

The energy needs of each individual are different, and recommendations for a healthy diet are often expressed as what proportion of energy should come from fat and carbohydrate (see *Fat* on the next page and *Carbohydrates* on page 22). The average amount of energy that a group of children of different ages between 1 and 5 are likely to need are summarised below.[1] (A more detailed breakdown of energy requirements by age and gender is given in Appendix 2.)

Age	Average energy requirements in kcals (calories) per day[1]
1 year	935kcals
2 years	1,160kcals
3 years	1,430kcals
4 years	1,530kcals
5 years	1,635kcals

The nutrients fat, carbohydrate and protein all provide the body with calories. (For more about these nutrients see pages 21-24.) At present, under-5s in the UK get most of their energy from carbohydrates (about 51%) and fats (about 36%), with protein providing about 13%.[2]

The proportion of energy that under-5s currently get from carbohydrate and fat meets the recommendations. However, more of the energy from carbohydrates should be provided by cereal foods, vegetables and potatoes, and less from confectionery and soft drinks as these foods are high in sugar but provide few other nutrients to the diet.

It is important to note that children do not need sugar for energy. (For more information about sugar and other carbohydrates, see pages 22-23.)

Fat

Fat in the diet

Fat provides the most concentrated form of energy in the diet.

There are basically two types of fat: saturated fats, which are mainly from animal sources; and unsaturated fats, which are found mainly in plants and fish. The unsaturated fats include a group called polyunsaturated fats.

Some fat in the diet is essential and the developing child has a particular need for what are known as 'essential fatty acids'. These are important for the development of brain and other tissues. Breast milk is relatively high in essential fatty acids to reflect this need. Fat in foods is also associated with the fat-soluble vitamins - vitamins A, D and E (see page 26).

How much fat should there be in children's diets? Are children getting too much?

Healthy eating recommendations for people aged over 5 are that total fat should provide no more than 35% of total food energy and that saturated fat should provide no more than 11% of food energy.[1] However, the amount of fat commonly eaten in the UK is far greater than requirements.

There is discussion about whether the above recommendations for the intake of fat in the diet (which are designed to reduce heart disease in the population) should also be applied to children under 5. The prevailing view is one of caution because there is concern that low fat intakes may have an adverse impact on children's growth and development. There is also concern that children who require a relatively nutrient-dense diet may not get enough nutrients if they are given low fat foods. For example, it is generally recommended that children under the age of 2 years are given whole milk and that skimmed milk is not given before 5 years of age.[9] The term 'muesli belt malnutrition' was coined to describe children from relatively affluent households who failed to grow and develop normally when given diets inappropriately low in fat.

However, it is accepted that the recommendations for adults are appropriate for the whole population from 5 years of age. Therefore, between infancy and 5 years there is an expectation that the proportion of energy derived from fat will fall from 50% (as supplied by breastfeeding) to 35% (as recommended for adults).

Children between the ages of $1^1/_2$ and $4^1/_2$ years in Britain currently appear to get about 35% of their energy from fat[2] and maintaining this level of total fat intake is to be encouraged as children get older.

The intake of saturated fat among those aged $1^1/_2$-$4^1/_2$ years is about 16% of food energy.[2] Although this is higher than the 11% recommended for people aged 5 years and over, this is to be expected since milk consumption in this group is high: almost a third of the saturated fat in the diets of under-5s is provided by milk.

Carbohydrates

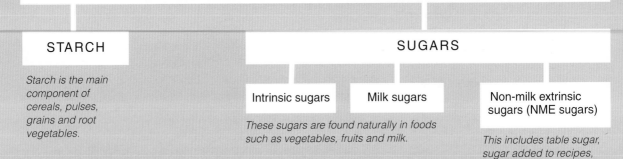

CARBOHYDRATES

STARCH

Starch is the main component of cereals, pulses, grains and root vegetables.

SUGARS

Intrinsic sugars

Milk sugars

These sugars are found naturally in foods such as vegetables, fruits and milk.

Non-milk extrinsic sugars (NME sugars)

This includes table sugar, sugar added to recipes, and honey.

Carbohydrates is the term used to describe both starch and sugars in foods. Carbohydrates provide energy.

Starch is the major component of cereals, pulses, grains and root vegetables. Most people can visualise starchy foods when they think of flour and potato.

The term 'sugars' is often assumed to describe something white and granular found in sugar bowls, but in fact the sugars found in foods can be quite variable. In order to clarify the roles of different sugars in health, the sugars in foods have been distinguished as: intrinsic sugars, milk sugars and non-milk extrinsic sugars (or NME sugars). Intrinsic and milk sugars are the sugars found naturally in foods such as milk, vegetables and fruits. NME sugars include table sugar, sugar added to recipes, and honey. NME sugars are found in foods such as confectionery, cakes, biscuits, soft drinks and fruit juices.

It is recommended that, for the population as a whole, carbohydrates should provide about 50% of total food energy, and that most of this should come from starch and intrinsic and milk sugars.[1] Children do not need 'sugars' for energy. They can get all the energy they need from other carbohydrate foods.

Starch, intrinsic sugars and milk sugars

How much do children need? Are they getting enough?

It is currently recommended that starch, intrinsic sugars and milk sugars together should provide about 40% of energy to the diet by the age of 5.[1] Starch, intrinsic sugars and milk sugars currently provide about 32% of energy in the diets of $1^1/_2$ - $4^1/_2$ year olds in Britain, of which about 10% is provided by milk sugars.[2] As milk intakes decline and appetites increase it is recommended that foods such as bread, potatoes, pasta and rice replace the energy no longer provided by milk. Starchy foods such as these fill children up, are a good source of energy and can also provide important nutrients such as fibre and some of the B vitamins.

Younger children who have smaller appetites may find starchy foods very filling, and a balance is required between the energy provided by starchy foods and that from other foods such as, for example, milk and meat (and products containing milk or meat) which may provide energy with less bulk.

Sources of starch and intrinsic and milk sugars

Sources of starch

Sources of starch include bread, rice, chapatis, pasta, breakfast cereals, potatoes, yams and plantains. Whole grain cereals are a valuable source of fibre (see page 25) but can be bulky and should be introduced gradually to the diets of under-5s.

Sources of intrinsic and milk sugars

Sources of intrinsic and milk sugars include fruits (but not fruit juices, see next page) and vegetables and milk.

Non-milk extrinsic sugars (NME sugars)

What are non-milk extrinsic sugars?

In the past, sugars were often referred to as 'added sugars' and 'natural sugars' - terms which many people found confusing. The Government's advisory panel COMA (Committee on Medical Aspects of Food and Nutrition Policy) defined different sugars in the diet more precisely depending on their effects on health. 'Non-milk extrinsic sugars' - or NME sugars - are those which have been extracted from a root, stem or fruit of a plant and are no longer incorporated into the cellular structure of food. NME sugars therefore include table sugar, sugar added to recipes, and sugars found in soft drinks and fruit juices. Honey is also included in this group.

The development of tooth decay is positively related to the amount and particularly the frequency of NME sugars in the diet.[10-12] This is most marked when sugar is eaten both at and between meals.

Sources of NME sugars

Sources of NME sugars include table sugar, honey, sweets, chocolate, cakes, biscuits, soft drinks, squashes and fruit juice. Soya infant formula also contains NME sugars (see page 44).

How much are children getting? Are they getting too much?

The recommendation to reduce the energy in the diet provided by NME sugars is primarily to prevent tooth decay.[1] The other concern is that foods high in NME sugars often provide calories but few other nutrients. This is particularly true for drinks such as squashes and fizzy drinks, sweets, and sugar added to drinks and cereals. Children need a relatively nutrient-dense diet. If a large proportion of the foods and drinks they consume are high in NME sugars, it may be difficult for under-5s to obtain all the nutrients they need each day.

The intakes of NME sugars among pre-school children in Britain are currently significantly higher than recommended. According to a national survey, children aged between $1^1/2$ and $4^1/2$ years in Britain obtain about 20% of their energy from NME sugars,[2] which is twice the current recommendation. (The contribution of NME sugars to the diet should be about 10% of total food energy.)[1] About 10% of the children in this survey were getting a third or more of their energy from NME sugars alone.

It is important to protect the first (milk) teeth of pre-school children so that these teeth stay in position to allow for the normal development of the permanent teeth. Pre-school children are considered at high risk for the development of tooth decay.[9]

When intakes of NME sugars are compared with dental health it has been shown that the consumption of sugary drinks at bedtime and frequent consumption of sugar confectionery and non-diet soft drinks are related to the amount of tooth decay.[13] For example, 40% of $3^1/2$ - $4^1/2$ year olds who had sugar confectionery most days, or more often, had experience of tooth decay, compared to 22% of those who had sugar confectionery less frequently.

It has also been reported that decay is more likely to affect pre-school children given first weaning foods containing sugar, those still drinking from a bottle at 2 years of age, and those who are given sweetened comforters (most commonly a sweet drink in a bottle or, less frequently, a dummy dipped in honey or jam).[14] In one study, just over 50% of children aged 1-5 years given a sweet comforter had severe tooth decay. It is therefore important not only to reduce the amount of NME sugars but also to reduce the frequency and the amount of contact that sugary foods and drinks have with the teeth.

The main sources of NME sugars among the under-5s are soft drinks (which contribute about a third of NME sugars), cereals and cereal products, and confectionery (which contribute about a quarter of NME sugars each) and table sugar itself which contributes about 5%.[2] Reducing the intake of soft drinks would have a major impact on the amount of NME sugars in many children's diets.

For more information about drinks for the under-5s and about dental health and practical ways to reduce tooth decay in the under-5s, see chapter 5.

Vitamins

Fat-soluble vitamins

Vitamin A
Vitamin D
Vitamin E

These are stored in the body.
Vitamin A can be destroyed by heat or by oxidation if left exposed to the air.

Water-soluble vitamins

B vitamins: thiamin, riboflavin, niacin
Vitamin B6
Vitamin B12
Folate
Vitamin C

These are not stored in the body and, because they are water-soluble, are also more likely to be destroyed by heat or by oxidation if left exposed to the air.

Vitamins are often divided into two groups: those that are water-soluble and those that are fat-soluble. Some vitamins are found predominantly or only in animal foods - for example vitamin B12 (only in animal foods), and vitamin D. Others are found predominantly in foods from vegetable origin - for example vitamin C.

The fat-soluble vitamins (A, D and E) are stored in the body and high doses of vitamins A and D should not be given.

Water-soluble vitamins (thiamin, riboflavin, niacin, vitamin B6, vitamin B12, folate and vitamin C) are not stored in the body and, because they are water-soluble, are also more likely to be destroyed if foods containing them are over-cooked or exposed to the air for long periods.

Reference Nutrient Intakes for the under-5s have been set for all vitamins except vitamin E. Not enough information is available at present to set a Reference Nutrient Intake for vitamin E.

It is important for children to get enough of each vitamin. However, having too much does not bring any benefit and may even be harmful.

Vitamin A (also known as retinol equivalents)

Why children need vitamin A

Vitamin A comes in two forms: retinol, which is only found in animal foods; and carotene, the yellow or orange pigment found in fruit and vegetables (both those coloured yellow or orange and in many green ones where the orange colour is masked by chlorophyll pigment). Carotene can be converted into retinol by the body; it takes 6 units of carotene to make 1 unit of retinol.

Vitamin A is often thought of as the 'anti-infection' vitamin as it plays an important role in maintaining the immune system. It is also essential for growth, which is why children have a relatively higher requirement for vitamin A than adults. Vitamin A is also associated with good vision in dim light as retinol is essential for the substance in the eye which allows night vision.

Experts now believe that carotene has a much wider role than just as a means to produce vitamin A. It may protect the body from internal damage which could lead eventually to heart disease or the development of cancer.

How much do children need? Are they getting enough?

Vitamin A is the most difficult vitamin to get right in the diets of children as both deficiency and excess can be a problem. Children aged 1-3 years have a Reference Nutrient Intake (RNI) for vitamin A of 400 micrograms a day and those aged 4-6 years of 500 micrograms a day[1] (see Appendix 2).

A national survey of children aged $1^1/_2$ - $4^1/_2$ years showed that almost half of all children had intakes below the Reference Nutrient Intake and 8% of children had very low intakes.[2] This may be due to the fact that only a limited number of foods are sources of vitamin A and many children are low consumers of vegetables. **For this reason, vitamin drops containing vitamin A are recommended for all under-5s.**

However, it is important not to give more vitamin drops than recommended because very high intakes of vitamin A can be dangerous. They can cause liver and bone damage, hair loss, double vision, vomiting and headaches.

It is recommended that regular intakes should not exceed 900 micrograms a day among infants, 1,800 micrograms a day among 1-3 year olds and 3,000 micrograms a day among 4-6 year olds. A normal diet and appropriate use of vitamin drops (5 drops a day) should give no cause for concern.

For information on vitamin drops see page 28.

Sources of vitamin A

Retinol

Few foods provide retinol naturally. The best sources are liver and liver pâté (since animals store vitamin A in the liver) although, as these foods can contain high levels of vitamin A, it is suggested that they are not given more than once a week.

Butter contains retinol as does cheese and to a lesser extent eggs. Margarine is fortified with vitamin A by law, and other fat spreads may also be fortified in this way. It is worth checking the label of other fat spreads to see if they are fortified. Milk and milk products usually provide about a third of daily vitamin A intakes in young children.

Carotene

Carrots are the best source of carotene but other orange foods such as sweet potatoes, mango, melon and apricots (dried or fresh) as well as green leafy vegetables (eg spinach, watercress, broccoli), tomatoes and red peppers are also good sources.

For more information on sources of vitamin A, see Appendix 1.

Vitamins (continued)

Vitamin D

Why children need vitamin D

Vitamin D is needed for healthy bones and teeth. Prolonged deficiency of vitamin D in children results in rickets, the main signs of which are skeletal malformation (eg bowed legs) with bone pain or tenderness and muscle weakness. A child with vitamin D deficiency is usually miserable and lethargic.

How much do children need? Are they getting enough?

The main source of vitamin D is by exposure of the skin to ultraviolet (UV) radiation in summer sunlight. Infants and children between 6 months and 3 years are particularly vulnerable to vitamin D depletion because of their rapid bone growth and the limited exposure some may have to UV radiation. Vitamin D is present in a limited number of foods and it is impossible for young children to obtain satisfactory vitamin D intakes from diet alone unless they take supplements.

After the age of 3 years people are generally able to maintain satisfactory vitamin D status from sunlight, so recommendations for intake are only made for children up to 3 years of age. The recommendation for infants and children aged between 7 months and 3 years is 7 micrograms of vitamin D a day.[1] **It is recommended that children up to 5 years of age receive supplementary vitamin D in vitamin drops.**[9] (See box below.)

There are concerns about the link between the exposure of the skin to UV radiation and subsequent skin cancer. The Health Education Authority recommends that young children should be protected from the sun by using shade and applying a high factor sunscreen on bare skin.[15] Using sunblocks on young children makes the use of vitamin D supplements especially important.

Under-5s of Asian origin are more likely to have lower vitamin D status. This may be due to a number of factors including a more limited exposure to the sun. Vitamin drops are particularly important for these children.

It is important not to exceed the recommended dose. High doses of vitamin D can be dangerous and the gap between the requirement and the toxic dose is not large. As little as five times the recommended intake taken regularly is associated with symptoms of vitamin D toxicity.

Sources of vitamin D

Very few foods are good sources of vitamin D. Oily fish such as tuna, salmon and pilchards provide vitamin D as do foods fortified by manufacturers such as margarine, many fat spreads, breakfast cereals, and some yoghurts and milk-based drinks. Infant formula, follow-on formula and many commercially available baby foods also contain vitamin D.

The main dietary sources of vitamin D among those aged $1^1/_2$ - $4^1/_2$ years are fat spreads and fortified breakfast cereals.[2]

For more information on sources of vitamin D, see Appendix 1.

Vitamin drops

The Department of Health recommends that children up to 5 receive vitamin supplements (vitamin drops) containing vitamins A, C and D. Vitamin drops are available free to families receiving Income Support or income-based Jobseeker's Allowance. Parents can get more information on vitamin drops from their Health Visitor or GP.

B vitamins: thiamin, riboflavin and niacin

Why children need the B vitamins thiamin, riboflavin and niacin

B vitamins are particularly important for the brain and nervous system. The body also needs these B vitamins - thiamin, riboflavin and niacin - to be able to use the energy (calories) in food.

How much do children need? Are they getting enough?

The Reference Nutrient Intakes for these vitamins are given in Appendix 2.

Average intakes of these vitamins are higher than the Reference Nutrient Intakes, with few children aged $1^1/_2$ - $4^1/_2$ years having intakes below those amounts.[2] However, those children with low intakes need particular attention.

A varied diet which provides sufficient energy and protein will usually provide enough of these vitamins at the same time.

Sources of thiamin and niacin

Sources of thiamin and niacin include: bread and other foods made with flour, breakfast cereals, pork (including bacon and ham), fish, yeast extract (eg marmite) and potatoes.

Sources of riboflavin

Sources of riboflavin include: milk and milk products such as yoghurt; poultry; meat; oily fish (such as tuna, salmon, sardines); and eggs. Milk and milk products provide about 50% of the daily riboflavin intakes for children aged $1^1/_2$ - $4^1/_2$ in Britain.[2]

For more information on sources of thiamin, riboflavin and niacin, see Appendix 1.

Folate

Why children need folate

Folates are a group of compounds, found in foods, which collectively are known as 'folate' or 'folic acid'.

Folate is an essential vitamin for many vital metabolic processes, and deficiency can lead to a particular type of anaemia known as megaloblastic anaemia.

How much do children need? Are they getting enough?

Accurate dietary assessment of folate is difficult, but intakes among children aged $1^1/_2$ - $4^1/_2$ years appear to be adequate.[2]

Children obtain over a third of their folate from cereal products, particularly breakfast cereals, about a fifth from vegetables, potatoes and snacks and almost a fifth from milk and milk products.[2]

Sources of folate

Sources of folate include green leafy vegetables and salads, oranges and other citrus fruits, liver and yeast extract as well as foods which have been fortified including breakfast cereals and some breads.

Folate is partly destroyed by prolonged heating, for example by overcooking food or by heating it and keeping it for long periods.

For more information on sources of folate, see Appendix 1.

Vitamins (continued)

Vitamin B6

Why children need vitamin B6

Vitamin B6 is the name given to a whole group of substances that are commonly found in both animal and vegetable foods and which are involved in a number of bodily processes involving amino acids (the protein building blocks).

How much do children need? Are they getting enough?

Deficiency is rare. If children have a varied diet they are unlikely to be deficient in B6.

Sources of vitamin B6

Good sources of vitamin B6 include liver, bananas, whole grain cereals and peanut butter.

Vitamin B12

Why children need vitamin B12

Vitamin B12 interacts with folate and vitamin B6. Together these vitamins help the body to build up its own protein, especially for nervous tissue and red blood cells.

How much do children need? Are they getting enough?

Vitamin B12 is found almost exclusively in animal products. Deficiency of this vitamin in under-5s is virtually unknown except when animal products are very strictly excluded from the diet.

Sources of vitamin B12

All foods of animal origin contain vitamin B12 - for example meat, fish and milk. Some other foods are fortified with vitamin B12, such as fortified breakfast cereals, drinks such as fortified blackcurrant drinks and some yeast extracts.

Five a day

Children (and adults) are advised to eat at least five portions of fruit or vegetables a day. Some examples of what this would mean for under-5s are given below.

a drink of apple juice (diluted)
a small banana
a portion of corn
a portion of peas
a bowl of tinned fruit

half an apple
a portion of carrots
a portion of broccoli
a drink of orange juice (diluted)
a small pack of raisins

Younger children may find it difficult to eat five portions of fruit and vegetables a day. However, it is important to offer young children different fruit and vegetables as this will encourage them to accept a wider variety of these foods and eat more fruit and vegetables as their appetite increases.

Vitamin C

Why children need vitamin C

Vitamin C has an important role in preventing disease and maintaining good health. The body needs vitamin C to produce and maintain collagen, the foundation material for bones, teeth, skin and tendons. It is also important in wound healing. It is suggested that vitamin C also has a role as an antioxidant vitamin in preventing damage to cells and tissues. Vitamin C also assists the absorption of iron in the diet if both nutrients are present in the same meal.

How much do children need? Are they getting enough?

The Reference Nutrient Intake for children over 1 year for vitamin C is 30mg a day.[1] In a national study of children aged 1¹/2 to 4¹/2 years,[2] 38% of children had intakes of vitamin C below the Reference Nutrient Intake.

Lower intakes were more likely to be reported in children of lower socio-economic status and children living in Scotland. These lower intakes are attributable to the lower intakes of fruit and vegetables, which are the major source of vitamin C.

Children currently obtain 50% of their vitamin C from soft drinks and fruit juice, with soft drinks (such as blackcurrant drinks) contributing 30% of vitamin C. Vegetables and potatoes contributed 19% of total vitamin C intake, 13% of which was from potatoes and savoury snacks. Fruit contributed only 15% of total daily vitamin C.

The under-5s in the UK currently eat too little fruit and vegetables and the variety is limited. The national study mentioned above found that peas and carrots are the vegetables most commonly eaten by the under-5s. Leafy green vegetables were eaten by less than 39% of children, and raw vegetables and salad eaten by less than a quarter of children during the 4-day study period. The average intake of all vegetable foods (excluding baked beans and potato) reported among children aged 1¹/2 - 4¹/2 years was 27g a day.[2] In the same survey fruit intake averaged 50g a day, two-thirds of which was apples and bananas. The recommendation to eat five portions of fruit and vegetables a day (see *Five a day* on the left) would ensure adequate vitamin C (and folate) intakes and would require average intakes of fruit and vegetables to increase.

It is important that fruit and vegetables are eaten every day as vitamin C cannot be stored in the body.

Sources of vitamin C

Sources of vitamin C include: fruit and fruit juices, potatoes (including chips) and other vegetables. Citrus fruits such as oranges are particularly good sources as are broccoli, green peppers, blackcurrants and strawberries. Some drinks are also fortified with vitamin C (see *Drinks for the under-5s* on page 44).

For more information on sources of vitamin C, see Appendix 1.

Minerals (continued)

Calcium

Why children need calcium

Calcium is required for building and maintaining bones, for the transmission of nerve impulses and muscle actions and for many other body functions.

How much do children need? Are they getting enough?

The current Reference Nutrient Intakes for calcium intake among children are:

- 350mg a day for 1-3 year olds, and
- 450mg a day for 4-6 year olds.[1]

The majority of children under 5 have adequate calcium intakes, with average intakes of about 600mg a day. About 50% of the calcium in the diets of under-5s comes from milk.[2] For more information about milk drinking in the under-5s see chapter 5.

It is important to ensure that children who do not have milk or dairy products have sufficient calcium, for example in a soya drink which has been fortified with calcium, or from tinned fish mashed with the bones. For more information about dairy-free diets, see chapter 5.

Sources of calcium

Sources of calcium include: milk, soya drink fortified with calcium, yoghurt, cheese, cheese spread, bread, tinned fish (eaten with the bones), tofu, egg yolk, and pulses such as beans, lentils and chick peas.

For more information on sources of calcium, see Appendix 1.

Zinc

Why children need zinc

Zinc plays a major role in the functioning of every organ in the body. It is needed for normal metabolism of protein, fat and carbohydrate and is associated with the hormone insulin which regulates the body's energy.

Zinc is also involved in the immune system, the utilisation of vitamin A, and in wound healing. Although it is known to have all those functions, more research is needed before the role of zinc can be defined more precisely.

How much do children need? Are they getting enough?

The Reference Nutrient Intakes of zinc are:
- 5mg a day for children aged 1-3, and
- 6.5mg a day for children aged 4-6 years.[1]

Lower intakes of zinc than these among children are frequently reported. In a national study of 1$\frac{1}{2}$ - 4$\frac{1}{2}$ year olds, more than 70% of children had intakes below the Reference Nutrient Intakes. A large proportion of children had very low intakes: 14% of under-4s and 37% of 4-6 year olds.[2]

A third of zinc in the diets of the under-5s is provided by milk and milk products, a quarter by cereals and cereal products, and a quarter from meat and meat products. The intake of zinc has been shown to go down relative to energy intake as children get older, and as the intake of milk declines.[2] An increase in the intake of meat and meat dishes will ensure a higher zinc intake. For those not eating meat, whole grain cereals and breakfast cereals, milk, milk products and eggs should be included regularly in the diet.

Sources of zinc

Sources of zinc include meat, eggs, milk, cheese, whole grain cereals and pulses.

Sodium

Sodium in the diet

Sodium is essential but too much can be potentially dangerous for young children. Their kidneys are not yet fully developed and cannot excrete excess amounts of sodium, which may accumulate and cause harm.

How much sodium do children need? Are they getting too much?

The main source of sodium in the diet is as salt (also called sodium chloride), added to manufactured foods and used in cooking and at the table. It is generally agreed that most people in Britain eat too much salt and there is evidence that this leads to raised blood pressure in later life.[1] Accustoming children to food which is salty early in life may encourage a lasting taste for salty foods.

Children who regularly eat snack foods such as crisps, processed meat (such as salami or ham), cheese and tinned foods such as beans or spaghetti in sauce, are probably getting far more salt than they need. There is certainly no need to add any salt to the diet of the under-5s in cooking or at the table.

Sources of sodium

Children should not eat foods which are high in sodium too often. Foods high in sodium include: bacon, ham, sausage, smoked cheese or smoked fish, crisps, salted snacks and some breakfast cereals.

Fresh meat and poultry and all fresh and frozen fruit and vegetables are low in sodium and are suitable for children.

Other minerals

A number of other minerals have a Reference Nutrient Intake and these are summarised briefly below.

Copper

Copper is an essential component of many substances which control bodily functions. Copper intakes have been found to be lower than the Reference Nutrient Intake among about a third of under-5s.[2] We do not yet know whether the health of those with low intakes is compromised. No tests are yet available to make this assessment. Copper is found in a wide variety of foods but is found particularly in vegetables, fish and liver.

Iodine

Iodine helps to make thyroid hormones necessary for maintaining the metabolic rate and in infants it is essential for the development of the nervous system. Iodine deficiency is now rare in the UK but is still common in many areas of the world, where infants born to mothers with severe iodine deficiency are likely to suffer mental retardation. Iodine is found in milk and fish in particular and intakes are generally in excess of requirements. Very high intakes can be toxic.

Magnesium

Magnesium is important for the development of the skeleton and for maintaining nerve and muscle function. The main sources of magnesium in the diet are cereals and green vegetables, with cereal foods providing about a third of daily magnesium intake.[2]

Minerals (continued)

Phosphorus

About 80% of the phosphorus in the body is present in the bones and phosphorus, with calcium, provides rigidity to the skeleton. Phosphorus is found in all plant and animal cells and therefore children will get enough phosphorus as long as they eat a varied diet.

Potassium

Potassium helps to regulate bodily fluids and also has a role in nerve and muscle function. It is therefore important for children to have an adequate intake. A large range of foods contain potassium and an inadequate intake is unlikely if children have a varied diet. Potassium is particularly abundant in vegetables, potatoes, fruit and juices.

Selenium

Selenium is involved in the mechanism which protects the body from damage inside the individual cells due to oxidation. There is little evidence to suggest that low intakes of selenium are associated with ill health in the UK. Selenium is found in cereals, meat and fish in particular, with cereals contributing about half of selenium intake in the UK.

Examples of good sources of vitamins and minerals in foods can be found in Appendix 1. Details of the Dietary Reference Values for all nutrients for under-5s are given in Appendix 2. For further information about under-5s' current intakes of energy and nutrients, see Appendix 3.

Chapter 4

Infant nutrition

This chapter summarises current advice on infant feeding and weaning. Infants are defined as those under the age of 12 months. Nutrition in the early years of life is a major determinant of growth and development and it may also influence adult health. Weaning - the introduction of solid foods to babies as they become less dependent on milk - coincides with a period of rapid growth and development, so a good diet during this period is crucial. Advice on infant feeding is largely based on recommendations from the Government Committee on Medical Aspects of Food and Nutrition Policy (COMA). For further sources of information, see Appendix 5.

Carers should support breastfeeding mothers and encourage them to continue providing breast milk.

Milk for babies

Infants up to 4-6 months of age receive all their nutritional requirements from breast milk or infant formula.

Breast milk

Breast milk is universally recognised as providing the best nutrition for babies. The balance of nutrients is uniquely ideal for a young baby and cannot be matched by a manufactured product. Also, it is easily digested, hygienic and contains antibodies that help babies to fight infections. Breast milk can provide the main drink throughout the first year of life.

Mothers who return to work but who wish to continue providing breast milk for their babies should be encouraged to do so. Advice on expressing and storing breast milk can be obtained from a Health Visitor or breastfeeding counsellor.

Advice for carers

- Carers should support breastfeeding mothers and encourage them to continue providing breast milk. Mothers who are breastfeeding and who may wish to feed their baby in the child care setting should have warm, private facilities made available to them.

- Expressed breast milk provided for babies in child care should be clearly labelled with the child's name and the date, stored in a refrigerator and only be used for that child. Any expressed milk left over at the end of the day should be returned to the parent or guardian.

See also *Giving bottle feeds* below.

Infant formula

There are a number of artificial milks available for babies called infant formula. These are usually based on cow's milk. If a baby is not being breast fed, only an appropriately modified formula baby milk can meet its nutritional needs. The advice given on the packet or tin must be followed. If there is any doubt about the suitability of the milk it is best to ask a Health Visitor for advice.

Infant formulas are usually manufactured from cow's milk but some are soya-based. Infant formula comes in two types: whey dominant or casein dominant (depending on whether casein or whey is the dominant protein). Whey dominant infant formula has a protein content adjusted to remove much more of

Giving bottle feeds

- Babies who are bottle fed should be held and have warm physical contact with an attentive adult while being fed.

- Babies should be fed by the same person at each feed.

- Babies should never be left propped up with bottles as this is both dangerous and inappropriate to babies' emotional needs.

- Bottles and teats for infants under 6 months of age should be thoroughly cleaned and sterilised. The teats of bottles for older infants should be thoroughly cleaned.

- Particular care should be taken if milk is heated in bottles. Ideally a bottle warmer should be used. If the bottle is heated by standing it in hot water, this should be done in an area which children do not have access to. A microwave should not be used to heat milk as the milk can become very hot even though the container still feels only warm.[1]

the casein from the cow's milk, which makes it a closer match to breast milk. Whey dominant formulas are usually suggested for very young babies. Casein dominant formulas are marketed as 'more satisfying' and many mothers change to these milks as their babies get older, although there is no firm evidence to suggest that these milks are more suitable.

Infant formula can be used as the main drink during the first year of life. From 6 months of age, follow-on infant formulas are also suitable as the main drink. Ordinary cow's milk is not suitable as a main drink before 12 months of age.

Advice for carers

- For those babies given infant formula it is essential that feeds are prepared correctly and safely. Parents of children who have infant formula should be encouraged to prepare their child's own feeds. Feeds should be labelled with the child's name, and the time and day the feed was made and should be stored in a refrigerator. Any infant formula left over at the end of the day should be returned to the parent or guardian.

- If the carer is making up infant formula, it is preferable if it can be made in a separate milk preparation area. The manufacturer's instructions for making up the infant formula should be followed carefully. This includes using the correct amount of powder and water, using only freshly boiled water (not bottled or sterilised water), and sterilising all equipment before use. Once prepared, it should not be stored for longer than 24 hours. Always discard the milk left in a bottle after a baby has finished feeding.

See also 'Giving bottle feeds' on page 37.

Timing of feeds

Because children in the first year of life are following individual feeding and sleeping patterns, it is recommended that these are not disrupted but wherever possible integrated into the carer's timetable for the day.

Weaning (starting on solid foods)

Up to the age of 4-6 months babies should be given only breast milk or infant formula which provides all the nutrients and fluid they need. There is no need to give solids or non-milk drinks before 4 months of age. Cooled boiled water is acceptable to quench thirst if the weather is exceptionally hot, but is not really necessary.

The age at which babies are ready for solid foods varies. From about 4 months of age, and if the baby seems ready to experiment, small spoonfuls of baby rice, puréed vegetables such as carrots or peas or mashed potato can be offered. If the food is rejected, go back to milk feeds only and try again at a later stage. By 6 months all babies should have started on solid foods. Parents of babies who were born prematurely need individual advice about when to start solid foods.

It is recommended that foods given to infants under 6 months of age are 'gluten-free' foods. Gluten is found in foods such as bread, pasta or chapatis made from wheat. Rice or oat cereals are acceptable and should be given from a spoon. Foods should not be added to bottles of milk as this may cause choking. Also, if the food is given in a drink the infant will not learn how food feels in the mouth or how to chew. Manufactured weaning foods (bought in packets, jars or tins) can be chosen according to the baby's age. It is important to offer a good variety of tastes so that infants get used to different flavours.

Peanuts in any form, including peanut butter, are not recommended before 6 months of age, and any child with a family history of allergy should not be given peanuts or peanut products in the first three years of life.[2]

One particularly important

One particularly important nutrient for babies is iron, as by 4-6 months the body stores of iron that an infant is born with have been used up, and the baby depends on obtaining iron from the diet.

Weaning tips

- Do not add salt to foods for infants.

- Do not give foods containing gluten (such as bread, pasta or chapatis) to infants under 6 months.

- Use naturally sweet fruits such as apples or bananas rather than adding sugar.

- Do not add artificial sweeteners to food for infants.

- Soft cooked meat, fish and pulses (such as peas, beans and lentils) are suitable foods to include in the diet from 4-6 months.

- Offer a variety of flavours and soft textures. Between 6 months and 1 year, give food which allows the infant to learn to chew and accept a wide variety of food textures.

- Eggs given to babies or toddlers should be cooked until both the yolk and the white are solid.

- If using commercial weaning foods, follow the manufacturer's instructions carefully.

- Whole cow's milk can be used as an ingredient in weaning foods, for example to moisten mashed potato, but cow's milk should not be the main drink for infants under 1 year.

- From 6 months, introduce foods with soft lumps, and finger foods.

Drinks for infants

- From 6 months of age, infants should be introduced to drinking from a cup or beaker. From the age of 1 year, they should be discouraged from drinking from a bottle.

- Adult-type soft drinks or 'diet' drinks, tea and coffee are not recommended for infants.

- Frequent use of fruit drinks, including baby juices and other baby drinks, should be discouraged as they encourage a sweet tooth and can contribute to dental disease.

- If drinks other than milk or water are given (for example diluted baby juices or baby drinks), these should be diluted with at least 8 parts water and confined to mealtimes. Because of the risk to dental health they should not be given in a feeding bottle.

Hygiene and safety tips

- If dummies or comforters are used they should be thoroughly cleaned and sterilised for infants under 6 months, and thoroughly cleaned for older infants. This also applies to dummies or comforters which are dropped.

- If you are serving food from a can or jar and the child is unlikely to eat all the contents, spoon a portion into a separate dish or container before serving it to the child. Store any unused portions according to the manufacturer's instructions. If there are no instructions, the safest option is to throw the unused portion away. If food is served straight from the jar and the child does not finish it, the remainder should be thrown away.

- Any uneaten food which parents have brought in should be returned to them at the end of the day.

- Do not use unpasteurised milk, or milk-based products such as cheese and yoghurt that are made from unpasteurised milk.

- Fruits and vegetables to be eaten raw should be well washed before eating. Carrots should be topped and peeled. Fruit and vegetables should be peeled for younger infants, to prevent choking.

- Whole pieces of nut should not be given to infants in case of choking.

- Never leave children or infants alone while they are eating in case they choke.

---

nutrient for babies is iron, as by 4-6 months the body stores of iron that an infant is born with have been used up, and the baby needs to obtain iron from the diet. (The importance of iron in the diet is discussed in detail on page 32.) Good sources of iron which can be given as purées or mash are: meat; fish such as tuna or sardines; pulses such as peas, beans and lentils; dried fruit; and green vegetables. The iron from meat and some fish is easily absorbed into the body and a daily helping of these foods is a valuable way of providing iron in the weaning diet.

Texture is also important. From about 6 months of age, children should be given food with soft lumps, or food which is mashed rather than puréed. As eating and chewing skills increase, minced or finely chopped foods and finger foods should be given and different textures of food should be introduced. By about 12 months, children should be getting a good mixed diet with three meals and two or three healthy snacks each day.

It is recommended that all infants under the age of 12 months should take a vitamin supplement (vitamin drops) containing vitamins A, C and D. Parents or guardians can get further information from their Health Visitor or GP.

Frequent use of fruit drinks, including baby juices and other baby drinks, should be discouraged as they encourage a sweet tooth and can contribute to dental disease.

Vitamin D and exposure to sunlight

Exposure to summer sunlight in outdoor play helps children to maintain their vitamin D status. However, child care settings should have a 'sun policy', with guidelines on how long children can remain outdoors in strong sunshine and on the use of protective clothing such as sunhats, and sunscreen. All under-5s should be appropriately supervised at all times while outdoors.

Recommendations

Drinks

- Breast milk is the best food for infants. Carers should support breastfeeding mothers and encourage them to continue providing breast milk. Mothers who are breastfeeding and who may wish to feed their baby in the child care setting should have warm, private facilities made available to them.

- If expressed breast milk is not provided, infants should be given an appropriate infant formula.

- Babies who are bottle fed should be held and have warm physical contact with an attentive adult while being fed. Babies should be fed by the same person at each feed.

- Babies should never be left propped up with bottles as this is both dangerous and inappropriate to babies' emotional needs.

- From 6 months of age, infants should be introduced to drinking from a cup or beaker, and from the age of 12 months, they should be discouraged from drinking from a bottle.

- Cow's milk is not suitable as a main drink for infants under 12 months. However, whole cow's milk can be used as an ingredient in weaning foods - for example to moisten mashed potato.

- If drinks other than milk or water are given - for example baby juices or baby drinks - these should be diluted with at least 8 parts water and should be confined to mealtimes. Because of the risk to dental health, children over 6 months should not be given these drinks in a feeding bottle. Water given to children under 6 months, either directly or in a diluted drink, should be boiled and cooled first.

- Adult-type soft drinks or 'diet' drinks, tea and coffee are not recommended for infants.

See also 'Dental health' on page 53.

Weaning (from 4-6 months)

- Foods containing gluten (such as bread, pasta or chapatis) should not be given to infants under 6 months.

- Salt should not be added to foods for infants.

- Naturally sweet fruits (such as apples or bananas) can be used to sweeten foods rather than adding sugar.

- Artificial sweeteners should not be added to foods for infants.

- Soft cooked meat, fish and pulses (for example peas, beans and lentils) are suitable foods to include in the diet from 4-6 months.

- It is important to offer a variety of flavours and soft textures. Between 6 and 12 months, food should be given which allows the infant to learn to chew and accept a wide variety of food textures.

- If using commercial weaning foods, follow the manufacturer's instructions carefully.

- Eggs given to babies or toddlers should be cooked until both the yolk and the white are solid.

- Because children in the first year of life are following individual feeding and sleeping patterns, it is recommended that these are not disrupted but wherever possible integrated into the carer's timetable for the day.

- It is recommended that children up to the age of 5 years should receive vitamin drops containing vitamins A, C and D. This is the responsibility of the parents or guardians but carers could provide information about where to find out more about them.

Food hygiene and safety issues for infants

- Expressed breast milk provided for babies in child care should be clearly labelled with the child's name and the date, stored in a refrigerator and only used for that child. Any expressed milk left over at the end of the day should be returned to the parent or guardian.

- Parents of children who take infant formula should be encouraged to prepare their child's own feeds. Feeds should be labelled with the child's name and the time and day the feed was made and should be stored in a refrigerator. Any infant formula left over at the end of the day should be returned to the parent or guardian.

- If the carer is making up infant formula, it is preferable if it can be made in a separate milk preparation area.

- Carers should take particular care if milk is heated in bottles. Ideally a bottle warmer should be used. If the bottle is heated by standing it in hot water, this should be done in an area which children do not have access to. A microwave should not be used to heat milk as the milk can become very hot even though the container still feels only warm.

- Bottles and teats for infants under 6 months of age should be thoroughly cleaned and sterilised. The teats of bottles for older infants should be thoroughly cleaned.

- If dummies or comforters are used they should be thoroughly cleaned and sterilised for infants under 6 months, and thoroughly cleaned for older infants. These recommendations also apply to dummies or comforters which are dropped.

- If the carer is serving food from a can or jar and the child is unlikely to eat all the contents, a portion should be spooned into a separate dish or container before serving it to the child. Any unused portions should be stored according to the manufacturer's instructions. (If there are no instructions, the safest option is to throw the unused portion away.) If food is served straight from the jar and the child does not finish it, the remainder should be thrown away.

- Any uneaten food which parents have brought in should be returned to them at the end of the day.

Chapter 5

Encouraging children to eat well

'Eating an apple on a sunny day.'
Rosa, aged 3½

Eating a variety of foods

The role of different nutrients in ensuring good health has been described in chapter 3. One of the basic principles to ensure healthy eating is to eat a variety of foods. It is easier to get all the vitamins and minerals needed for good health if a good variety of foods is eaten. It is difficult to achieve adequate intakes of vitamins and minerals when diets are monotonous and based on few foods,[1] and a varied diet is associated with better health.[2]

Children do not have an inborn ability to select a balanced and nutritious diet[3] but increasing the variety of available foods should increase the number of different foods chosen.[4]

As children get older they are generally willing to eat a wider

One of the basic principles to ensure healthy eating is to eat a variety of foods. It is easier to get all the vitamins and minerals needed for good health if a good variety of foods is eaten.

variety of foods, and snacks become an increasingly important source of energy and nutrients. The innate preference for foods which are sweet is particularly observed in childhood. Children who are consistently exposed to sweet tastes may reject other tastes.

There are some vitamins and minerals which have been shown to be consumed by children in amounts below the Reference Nutrient Intakes. These include vitamins A and C and the minerals iron and zinc. Increasing the amounts of different meats, cereals and fruit and vegetables in the diet is likely to improve the intake of all these nutrients. Diets which are not varied are often particularly low in fruit and vegetable foods. A low intake of these foods is associated with poverty.[1]

Fruit and vegetables are now thought to be particularly important for good health. In adults the antioxidant nutrients they contain probably protect against chronic diseases such as coronary heart disease and cancer. Along with the rest of the population, under-5s should be encouraged to eat five portions of fruit and vegetables a day*.[5] Children could have child-sized portions, for example: half an apple, sliced; 2 portions of vegetables (such as peas, carrots or tomatoes); 1 glass of fruit juice (diluted, and preferably served with a meal); and a small banana or dried fruit snack (eg raisins). (See page 30 for other examples of 'five a day'.)

It is worth experimenting with different vegetables and vegetable dishes to find those that are acceptable. Some children may reject cabbage but enjoy 'bubble

and squeak' (cabbage and potato mixed together). Others may find stir-fry vegetables more interesting than boiled ones. Carrots, red peppers and sweetcorn are appealing in colour, taste and texture. Peas are a popular and familiar vegetable for most children. Some children like raw vegetables more than cooked ones.

Parents and carers often allow a child's initial rejection of a new food to determine whether that food is offered again, yet research has shown that continued exposure to a food will increase the likelihood that the child will eventually eat it.[6] It has been shown however that a new food will not be chosen unless the child has tasted it, which suggests that it is important to encourage children to taste all the foods offered at a meal.[7] Parents or guardians, particularly those on low incomes, may be unwilling to experiment with new foods which may be rejected and then thrown away. Carers can often offer a wider choice and may play an important part in encouraging a varied diet.

It is important that foods offered to children as snacks are also varied. Although biscuits and crisps are eaten regularly by about 80% of children between 1¹/₂ - 4¹/₂ years,[8]

> **Parents or guardians, particularly those on low incomes, may be unwilling to experiment with new foods which may be rejected and then thrown away. Carers can often offer a wider choice and may play an important part in encouraging a varied diet.**

these are not the only or the most nutritious snacks available. Snack foods can be based on a variety of cereals and cereal products as well as on fruits and vegetables. Some ideas for a variety of different snack foods are given on page 47.

Physical activity

Physical activity is a term used to describe body movement. It includes:

- everyday body movements such as walking, playing, or climbing stairs, and

- movement which is often described as 'exercise'. For children this might be, for example, running, playing football, or playing in a playground.

The more the body moves, the more energy (or calories) is used up. The relationship between energy (calorie) intake and physical activity is explained on page 20.

Activity can be encouraged both indoors and outdoors. Outdoor play gives children the opportunity to 'let off steam' and provides many more opportunities for them to be physically active. Most children are attracted to outdoor play if they are offered a range of suitable activities.

The Health Education Authority recommends that all young people should participate in physical activity of at least moderate intensity (enough to make them feel

---

Eating a varied diet

Children should be encouraged to eat a varied diet. They should eat foods from each of the four main food groups every day. The four main food groups are:

- bread, other cereals and potatoes

- fruit and vegetables

- milk and dairy foods, and

- meat, fish and alternatives such as pulses (peas, beans and lentils), and soya.

A varied diet is associated with better health as it is more likely to contain all the vitamins and minerals the body needs.

---

* Potatoes are a good source of starch but are not included in the 'five a day' advice.

Why it is important for children to be physically active

• The more energy children use up, the more food they will need to eat. A child who is inactive may have a very small appetite and may not be able to get all the nutrients he or she needs in a small amount of food.

• Exposure to summer sunlight in outdoor play helps children to maintain their vitamin D status (see page 28).

• Physical activity builds up muscle strength and overall fitness, and develops physical skills such as balance, coordination and climbing skills.

• A considerable amount of learning can take place while children are playing outdoors. For example, they learn about the environment around them, and interacting with other children can contribute to their confidence.

• Children who develop an active lifestyle and enjoy physical activities when they are young, are more likely to maintain that healthy lifestyle in adult life. An active lifestyle reduces the risk of ill health in adulthood.

warm and slightly out of breath) for an average of at least half an hour and preferably one hour a day at 5 years of age.[9]

It is essential that there is outdoor space where children can play, or access to an outside area such as a garden, park or other safe open space. Carers need to timetable periods of activity into the children's daily routine and encourage children to be active throughout the year. Children in child care should also have access to toys for active play - for example balls, hoops and skipping ropes.

Carers should ensure that outdoor play equipment is safe. All children should be closely supervised during sand and water play and should not be left alone while playing outdoors.

Carers should be aware that some children's dress may restrict them in outdoor play and it may be necessary to sensitively adjust their clothing for outdoor activities. Children playing outside should be appropriately dressed for cold or rainy weather with coats and jackets buttoned up and scarves, mittens, boots and hats used as necessary.

Exposure to summer sunlight in outdoor play helps children to maintain their vitamin D status. However, child care settings should have a 'sun policy', with guidelines on how long children can remain outdoors in strong sunshine, and on the use of protective clothing such as sunhats, and sunscreen.

Food for all

Food is an important part of everyone's lives. Eating together, having special foods and avoiding particular foods are all intimately related to aspects of people's family life, cultural, religious and intellectual beliefs. It is important to recognise that food available for any group of people should be appropriate and familiar. It is essential to involve parents or guardians in the choice of foods provided in child care: good communication between parents and those providing child care is vital.

When planning meals for any group of people, the particular needs of that group must be considered. Cultural and religious differences are commonly expressed in food preferences and food avoidances. Providing the right ingredients is not the only factor to consider: food should look and taste familiar as well.

All food activities should allow for cultural differences: activities involving food give children the opportunity to learn about new and different foods. Holidays, festivals and religious celebrations of various cultures provide a valuable opportunity to celebrate differences in food experiences.

Some of the differences in food choice commonly observed by those from different religious and cultural groups are summarised in Appendix 4. It is important to emphasise that there may be individual differences in food choices between families, and those providing child care should not make assumptions about anyone's food preferences. It is important to find out about each child from his or her parent or guardian.

All children, and their parents or guardians, should be respected as individuals, and their food preferences and religious requirements should be accommodated.

All that children bring with them to their place of child care - their race, gender, family background, language, culture and religion - should be valued in order for children to feel accepted and accepting of themselves. It is therefore important to value the contributions which different cultures and nationalities make to the variety of foods eaten in the UK today.

Drinks for the under-5s

Milk

Milk is the main source of calcium for the under-5s and it also contributes substantially to the protein, riboflavin, vitamin A and zinc intakes of children in this age group. Children aged between 12 months and 2 years should be given whole milk. Semi-skimmed milk can be introduced gradually after the age of 2 years, provided that the child is a good eater and has a varied diet.

Skimmed milk is not suitable as a main drink for children under 5 years of age, as it does not contain enough calories or vitamins.

Some children may reject milk unless some flavouring is added. Flavoured milk is usually sweetened in some way and, while this may be a useful way of encouraging milk drinking in some children, it is better that flavoured sweetened drinks are drunk with meals, rather than between meals, because of the risk to teeth.

Some children cannot drink cow's milk and this may be substituted with goat's milk or soya drinks. Some of the alternative milks available are described on the right.

The Welfare Food Scheme enables children under 5 to receive a third of a pint (almost 200ml) of milk (whole or semi-skimmed) free of charge on each day if they attend approved day care facilities (which includes nurseries, pre-schools and registered childminders) for two hours or more. Providers can apply direct to the Welfare Food Reimbursement Unit* (WFRU) to participate in the scheme. Some local authorities administer the scheme centrally on behalf of some pre-schools. This provision is in addition to the milk tokens scheme** for parents on Income Support or Jobseeker's Allowance.

*To obtain a copy of Welfare Food Scheme - Nursery Milk Guide: For Providers of Day Care for Children Under Five, write to: the Section Manager, Welfare Food Reimbursement Unit, PO Box 1, Corby, Northants NN17 1GX.

** For a copy of Welfare Milk and Vitamins: A Guide for Families, write to: Department of Health, PO Box 410, Wetherby LS23 7LN.

Which milks to give under-5s as a main drink

Infants = children under 12 months

Breast milk	The best milk for infants.
Infant formula	Cow's milk specially modified for infants is labelled as such. Follow the instructions given on the packet or tin when choosing and preparing infant formula.
Follow-on infant formula	Modified cow's milk suitable for infants from about 6 months of age.
Soya infant formula	May be given from birth, especially if advised by a doctor. These formulas contain sugar in the form of glucose which is more harmful to teeth than the lactose in infant formula based on cow's milk. Care should be taken that infants are not left with bottles for long periods and children should be given soya infant formula in cups, preferably with meals.
Whole cow's milk*	Not suitable for infants. Suitable for most children from 12 months of age.
Semi-skimmed cow's milk*	Not suitable for infants or children under 2 years, but can be introduced gradually after the age of 2 years, provided that the child is a good eater and has a varied diet.
Skimmed cow's milk*, including dried skimmed milks	Not suitable for infants or children under 5 years.
Evaporated milk	Not suitable for infants. Skimmed milk varieties are not suitable for children.
Condensed milk	Not suitable for infants or children.
Soya drinks (other than soya infant formula)	Not suitable for infants. If children are given soya drinks, make sure the drink is calcium-fortified. Drinks should be given in cups at mealtimes, because of the sugars content.
Goat's milk*	Not suitable for infants unless recommended by a Paediatrician.
Oat drinks	Not suitable for children as they are not fortified with calcium.

* Milks given to under-5s should be pasteurised.

Soft drinks

There is a wide range of soft drinks available, most of which are sweetened with sugars, sweeteners (for example saccharin or aspartame) and commonly a mixture of both. They include:

- squashes and other drinks which need to be diluted
- carbonated soft drinks such as cola or lemonade, and
- fruit drinks which are drinks that contain a proportion of fruit juice

as well as water and some form of sugar and/or sweetener.

Children can be conditioned at an early age to the sweet taste of drinks. High intakes of soft drinks have been reported to lead to frequent looser stools, poor appetites and failure to thrive, as well as poorer behaviour and co-operation at mealtimes.[10]

Soft drinks containing sweeteners are generally not recommended for children. If soft drinks (such as squashes) containing saccharin are given to the under-5s they should be diluted much more than they would be for an adult - for example, a dilution of 1 part squash to at least 8 parts water.

Soft drinks containing sugar can be harmful to the teeth, especially if they are drunk frequently or stay in contact with the teeth for too long. If sugary drinks are given they should be kept to meal times. Soft drinks such as fruit drinks and fruit squashes should not be given at bedtime or during the night as this practice is particularly associated with dental decay.

Soft drinks labelled 'low sugar' or 'no added sugar' may still harm children's teeth as they often do contain some sugar and they may also be acidic. This is also true for baby herbal drinks. Any of the following on the label of a soft drink indicates that the drink has sugar added: glucose, glucose syrup, fructose, concentrated fruit juice, sucrose, dextrose, honey, invert sugar, maltose, hydrolysed starch.

Sweetened fizzy drinks such as cola or lemonade are both sugary and acidic. The 'diet' versions of these drinks can also be harmful to teeth even if they do not contain sugar, as the acidity erodes the dental enamel.

Many ready-to-drink cartons of squashes, fruit drinks or fruit juices have a high sugar content and cannot be diluted and children regularly given full strength drinks may become used to the intensity of the sweetness. Children who bring their own drinks to child care should be encouraged to bring a plastic flask or a lidded plastic cup containing an appropriately diluted drink.

Fruit juices

Pure fruit juices are a good source of vitamin C. They are most beneficial when given with meals, as this helps the body absorb iron. However, fruit juices have also been shown to be acidic enough to erode dental enamel in young children so when giving them to under-5s it is best to dilute them with plenty of water.

Some fruit juices which have been fortified with a range of extra vitamins and minerals are not suitable for children. Check the label to see if the drink is marked 'unsuitable for children'.

Encourage children to drink water if they are thirsty. Water quenches thirst, does not spoil the appetite, and does not damage teeth.

Other drinks

Tap water is suitable for children: some bottled waters may have a high content of salts.

Tea and coffee are not recommended as a drink for infants or children as the tannic acid they contain reduces the absorption of iron. However, it is recognised that some children in child care are given milky tea as a way of encouraging them to drink milk. If tea is used in this way it should be very weak.

Which drinks to give

- Encourage children to drink water if they are thirsty. Water quenches thirst, does not spoil the appetite, and does not damage teeth. Tap water may be preferable as some bottled waters have a high content of salts and may not be suitable.

- Promote milk as a drink. Whole cow's milk is suitable as a main drink for most children from 12 months of age. Semi-skimmed milk can be introduced after the age of 2 years, provided that the child is a good eater. Skimmed milk is not suitable as the main drink for a child under 5 years of age.

- Diluted fruit juice is a useful source of vitamin C. Children should be encouraged to have a glass of diluted fruit juice with their main meal or with breakfast as this may also help the body to absorb iron (see chapter 3).

- Discourage children from having fizzy drinks and squashes (including fruit squashes), both diet and non-diet, as these can erode the tooth enamel and contribute to tooth decay. Also, they provide little in the way of nutrients, and children who drink them frequently may have less appetite to eat well at mealtimes.

- Tea and coffee are not suitable drinks for under-5s as they contain tannic acid which interferes with iron absorption.

Promote milk as a drink. Whole cow's milk is suitable as a main drink for most children from 12 months of age.

Dental health among the under-5s

The role of non-milk extrinsic sugars (NME sugars) in dental health is described in chapter 3. It is accepted that dental decay is directly related to the frequency and amount of NME sugar consumption.[11] There is a popular myth that it does not matter if children have tooth decay in their first teeth. This is not the case. Tooth decay in a child's first teeth:

- can affect the development of the permanent teeth
- can be painful, and
- may involve the need to extract teeth under anaesthetic.

How carers can help reduce tooth decay in children

- Reduce the total amount and especially the *frequency* of sugary foods and drinks that children have.

- If children are having sugary foods and drinks, these should be given with meals rather than between meals. This is because children's first teeth are prone to decay if they are frequently in contact with sugars.

- To help the healthy development of teeth, children should not be given sweet drinks (such as fruit juice, squashes and other soft drinks) in a feeding bottle or dinky feeder. A cup or beaker should be used if these drinks are given with meals.

- If a child uses a dummy or comforter, do not dip it into sugar or sugary drinks as this can contribute to tooth decay.

- Some soft drinks which claim to have 'no added sugar' still contain sugars which are harmful to the teeth. Diet drinks, both fizzy and still, can also be harmful to the teeth. This is because they may be acidic and erode the dental enamel, especially if sipped frequently. The use of these drinks should be avoided or limited.

Additional advice for parents of under-5s

- Brush children's teeth daily with a pea-sized blob of fluoride toothpaste.

- Fluoride supplements can be given to children who are at high risk of dental decay. Parents should ask their child's dentist if this is necessary.

- Children should start visiting the dentist regularly by 3 years of age. (Dental check-ups and treatment are free up to the age of 18, or up to 19 if they are in full-time education.)

- Choose sugar-free medicines where possible. If a GP is prescribing medicines, the parent should ask the GP or pharmacist if a sugar-free version is available.

- Soft drinks such as fruit drinks and fruit squashes should not be given at bedtime or during the night as these are particularly associated with dental decay.

Parents and guardians should work together with carers to ensure that children have breakfast, either at home or when they arrive in child care.

Eating patterns and timing of meals and snacks

The eating patterns of many pre-school children are erratic and food faddiness is common. Children at this age become rapidly disgruntled when hungry and are likely to require snacks in between their main mealtimes.

If children in child care are given snacks either at inappropriate times or inadequately, they may be ravenous when picked up by their parents or guardians. They may then fill up with snack foods on the way home, which do not provide the same nutritional benefit as a main meal. Carers and parents or guardians may wish to discuss the most appropriate times for afternoon snacks and tea so that this can be avoided.

Breakfast

Children who are cared for outside the family home may have less time for breakfast at home and may benefit from a meal similar to breakfast with their carer. Breakfast cereals served with full-fat milk make an important contribution to daily nutrient intakes. The best breakfast cereals for children are those which do not have sugar added and which are often fortified with minerals and vitamins (particularly iron) - for example cornflakes, crisped rice, puffed wheat or wheat bisks. Higher fibre cereals (such as whole grain or bran cereals) should be given in moderation as they are bulky and may fill children up quickly. Cereals (such as muesli) which contain whole nuts should not be given to the under-5s.

It is important that children have breakfast. Parents and guardians should work together with carers to ensure that children have breakfast, either at home or when they arrive in child care.

Timing of meals

Children need to eat regularly and it is recommended that children are offered something to eat at least every three hours.

Some children may eat slowly. It is important to ensure that all children have enough time to eat.

Snacks

Children need nutritious snacks between meals. The best snacks are those which are low in added sugar. A variety of snacks should be offered including fruit, vegetables and any type of bread such as sandwiches, teacakes or fruit buns (see box below). It is best to avoid giving sweets, sweet biscuits, sugary or fizzy drinks and fruit juices as snacks: keep these foods and drinks to mealtimes only.

Carer involvement in meals

To help develop social skills, it is good practice for carers to sit with children when they are eating and (where appropriate and if they can), eat the same foods and drink the same drinks. An encouraging and pleasant environment is important at meals and carers can provide a positive role model.[7] In the same way as carers should not smoke in front of children, they should also set a good example in the foods and drinks they choose for themselves.

A meal is a time for eating but it should also be a time for socialising and learning. Children can learn from the carer about table manners, and can practise their speaking and listening skills. To encourage this, distractions such as television are best avoided during mealtimes. All children should be encouraged to do whatever they can for themselves in terms of eating to help them develop skills and independence. Encouraging good table manners and social skills around eating are an important part of a child's development.

Language development is fostered when children interact in small groups and carers should sit and chat with children during meals and snacks. Children also enjoy being involved in meal preparation, table setting and clearing away.

Rewards are often given to children as a way of encouraging good behaviour or if they have done well in a particular task. Rather than giving sweets, chocolates and sweet snacks such as biscuits to reward good behaviour, rewards can be given in the form of smiles and praise ('soft rewards') or as small inexpensive items such as stars, stickers or badges ('hard rewards'). Most children are very happy with soft rewards and enjoy getting praise or attention. Older children are more likely to be influenced by hard rewards but a simple stamp on the hand with washable ink (for example in the shape of a teddy) will allow the child to see and share their 'reward' with parents and guardians.

There is nothing wrong with giving children sweets occasionally and children will often receive them as tokens of affection or to celebrate special events such as Easter, Chinese New Year or Diwali. It is best to give sweets after a main meal rather than between meals as they will do the least damage to teeth at this time and will not spoil the child's appetite.

Ideas for nutritious snacks

- Dairy foods such as cheese or plain yoghurt with added fruit

- Fresh fruit

- Dried fruit such as raisins or dried apricots

- Raw vegetables such as peeled carrots, sweet pepper, tomato, cucumber or celery (all well washed)

- Home-made plain popcorn

- Low sugar breakfast cereals

- Plain biscuits such as rich tea, oatcakes, breadsticks, cream crackers, matzos, rice waffles, melba toast or crispbread

- Any type of bread including fruit bread, crumpets, teacakes, muffins, fruit buns, malt loaf, bagels, pitta bread or sandwiches. Suitable fillings for sandwiches might be meat (for example chicken, ham, corned beef, meat paste), cheese, yeast extract, fish paste, tuna, egg, banana, salad or combinations of these.

Ideas for nutritious snacks are also included in the sample menus given in chapter 6.

Making the most of mealtimes

- Sit with the children during meals and snacks.

- If the carer eats at the same time as children, it is important that what the carer eats and drinks provides a good role model for healthy eating.

- Avoid distractions such as television.

- Do not hurry children as they eat.

- Encourage children to try all the food offered to them.

- Encourage good table manners.

- Do not force children to eat all the food offered.

- Chat to the children during the meal.

- Use the mealtime as an opportunity to provide education about healthy eating.

- Respect the behavioural norms and expectations of specific cultures.

Adapted from Nahikan-Nelms. See reference 7.

Involving parents and guardians

It is important to involve parents or guardians in encouraging healthy eating. A real partnership between carers and parents and guardians should be fostered. This could include:

- Meeting with parents or guardians and making sure they are aware that the carers are committed to providing healthy, varied (and enjoyable) food.

- Making menus available to parents, for example by displaying them on a noticeboard, or where children leave their coats. This will help families to plan a diet which is balanced between the child care setting and home. Carers could also ask parents for suggestions for menu items.

- Giving parents adequate notice of any changes to meals, food choice or any other aspect of food provision, and allowing them to comment on and discuss the changes before they are introduced.

- Giving parents or guardians clear information each day about what food has been eaten and if their child has eaten well. Even older children may not be accurate in reporting what they have eaten.

- Inviting parents and guardians to share special foods and recipes with carers. Carers should seek advice from parents and guardians if they are serving food which the carers themselves are not familiar with. Such food should not only contain the right ingredients but should look and taste right too.

Carers should ask parents or guardians about any special dietary requirements their child has before the child starts attending the child care setting. Parents or guardians of children who are on special diets (for example a gluten-free diet) or who have food intolerances are responsible for providing the carer with information about the food choices available to their child. Parents should talk to their GP or Health Visitor for help and advice. The GP may refer the family to a State Registered Dietitian. In some cases, the carer may want to insist that the parent or guardian provides the child's food, for example for children on vegan diets.

Dealing with food refusal

Children should be allowed to make their own food choices. If a child refuses a food or meal, the carer should gently encourage them to eat, but children should never be forced to eat. To minimise food refusal, it is important to ensure that a variety of foods are offered.

If a child refuses a food even after gentle encouragement to eat, remove the food without making a fuss or passing judgement. While it is useful to encourage children to try different foods, it is not good practice to reward children for eating food they do not want (particularly by the reward of pudding or a sweet snack). Words of praise and encouragement to try foods and eat a variety of foods may help some children at mealtimes. It may be useful to adopt the approach that a food refused is 'not liked today'. Food fads often do not last more than a couple of weeks and children may, at another time, accept a food that was previously rejected. It is important that a good variety of foods are continually offered.

While it can be distressing for carers (and parents or guardians) to have food they have prepared rejected, keeping your own attitude to eating friendly and relaxed will help children to feel that eating is a pleasurable way to satisfy hunger rather than a battleground.

A child's opinion about what they like and dislike should be respected and it is better not to 'disguise' foods that they have rejected. Changing the form a food is given in however may make a food more acceptable. For example, a child might refuse cooked carrots but enjoy raw ones or may refuse pasta coated in sauce but prefer the pasta and sauce served separately.

Food intolerances

In food allergy there is an abnormal sensitivity to a substance present in food which is generally considered harmless for the majority of people. Foods that can cause severe reactions include: peanuts, nuts, shellfish, sesame seeds, cow's milk, eggs, fish, citrus fruits, soya beans, wheat and other cereals. Food allergies are more likely to occur in children with a family history of allergies such as asthma, eczema or hay fever.

While many parents believe that their children are sensitive to certain foods, the true incidence is likely to be very much lower than reported. Parents requesting special diets for their children because of food allergy should be encouraged to seek advice from a doctor or State Registered Dietitian if they have not already done so. It is unwise to restrict food choice among young children without appropriate help and advice.

However, it is important to note that a Department of Health Expert Panel recommends that, in children with a family history of atopic disease (asthma, eczema, hay fever or food allergy), peanuts and peanut products should be avoided until the child is 3 years old.[12]

Vegetarian diets

It is possible for a child to get the energy and nutrients he or she needs from a vegetarian diet but a little extra care is needed. Nutrient-rich foods such as milk, cheese and eggs can provide protein, vitamin A, calcium and zinc but obtaining enough iron from a meat-free diet may be more difficult. If the child eats fish, iron can be found in oily fish such as sardines, pilchards and tuna. Iron is also found in pulses such as beans and lentils, in dried fruit and in breakfast cereals. The iron is more easily absorbed if the child has foods or drinks that are high in vitamin C - for example fruits, vegetables or juices - at the same meal. Tea and coffee should not be given as these can interfere with the absorption of iron. A vegetarian diet which provides a variety of cereal foods, vegetables, pulses, fruits and dairy products is likely to supply sufficient nutrients.

A vegetarian diet which provides a variety of cereal foods, vegetables, pulses, fruits and dairy products is likely to supply sufficient nutrients.

The vitamin drops obtained at Child Health Centres are not derived from animal sources, so they are appropriate for vegetarians.

When cooking food for vegetarians who exclude food items for religious or ethical reasons, it is important that food given is not compromised in any way. For example, picking meat out of a dish is not acceptable - the vegetarian dish should be prepared first and the meat added later for other children.

Vegan diets

Vegan diets are outside the scope of this report. Parents of vegan children must take their own responsibility for their children's diets and can get advice from The Vegetarian Society or The Vegan Society (see Appendix 5).

Dairy-free diets

Dairy-free diets may be necessary for children who are lactose intolerant. (Lactose is the sugar naturally occurring in milk and all milk-based foods.) Lactose intolerance is commonly found in some Asian and African populations, and is caused by a deficiency of lactase, the enzyme required to digest lactose. Lactose intolerance causes unpleasant digestive symptoms including diarrhoea. More rarely, children may be intolerant to cow's milk protein.

Milk and other dairy foods provide a substantial amount of calcium and riboflavin in the diets of children.

Infants and children up to 2 years who do not have milk or dairy products should continue on the infant formula recommended to them by a doctor or State Registered Dietitian. After the age of 2, if soya products are acceptable, children can be given a soya drink which has been fortified with calcium (found by checking the label). Other sources of non-dairy calcium are soya-based foods such as tofu, tempeh and soya mince or soya cheese, canned sardines or salmon (including the bones), egg yolk, bread, breakfast cereals, pulses (such as beans, lentils and chick peas), dark green leafy vegetables, and dried fruit.

Special diets

Some children have special dietary requirements. Special diets are the foods recommended by a State Registered Dietitian or doctor for a specific medical condition. Children with coeliac disease for example cannot tolerate gluten, the protein in wheat flour, and require a gluten-free diet. If a child has a recognised special diet, the parent or guardian should be able to supply a list of acceptable foods, and in some cases can provide the foods themselves.

For children who are advised to avoid nuts in foods, careful checking of food labels will be required. The following are some of the names given to nuts or nut products: nuts, chipped nuts, flaked nuts, peanuts, groundnuts, monkey nuts, earthnuts, arachis hypogaea, arachis oil, groundnut oil, peanut oil, peanut butter, nut butters, nut paste, marzipan, praline, frangipane, goober peas, pinder, goober, nut flavours, nut extract, hydrolysed vegetable oils or proteins, nut oil derivatives or additives such as E471, E472 or lecithin.

The nut content of some foods may be too small to warrant labelling but enough to cause a severe reaction in an allergic child. A careful plan for choosing a safe and nutritious diet for the individual child needs to be drawn up in consultation with a State Registered Dietitian.

For children who are milk intolerant all foods containing milk and milk products should be avoided and the parent or guardian should be able to provide a list of foods which are milk product free.

Special diets can be quite complex but parents should be able to provide enough information about their child's specific needs to enable a carer to provide the right food. Help and advice in providing suitable meals and snacks for those with medically necessary dietary restrictions can be obtained from a State Registered Dietitian. The GP may be able to refer the family to one.

Children with special needs

When planning food provision and menus, carers need to consider children who have special needs. Some children may have particular dietary requirements or may need specific help with eating, both of which are outside the scope of this report. Advice can be obtained from a State Registered Dietitian. Parents or guardians and carers may also find it useful to contact support groups associated with the child's particular disability or need.

Food safety and good hygiene

Food provided to under-5s should be stored, prepared and presented in a safe and hygienic environment. Extra care is needed for infants and young children as they may have a lower resistance to food poisoning.

Carers should always wash their hands with soap and water before preparing food or helping children to eat, and after changing nappies and toileting children. If carers use a handkerchief while preparing food, they should wash their hands before continuing.

Carers need to be aware of the requirements of the Food Safety Act. Some carers may need to complete a Food Hygiene Certificate course. Further information on this can be obtained from the local authority's environmental health department, or from its registration and inspection unit.

Carers also need to be aware of food hygiene and food safety to prevent food contamination and food poisoning. They need to know about storage of food and leftover food, and thorough cooking or heating of foods. Several useful publications are available from the Ministry of Agriculture, Fisheries and Food (see Appendix 5). Carers should obtain and follow the advice in these. Some of the main points for carers are given in the box below.

It is also important that children are taught basic hygiene themselves - for example not eating food that has fallen on the floor, washing their hands with soap and water before eating meals or snacks and after going to the toilet or handling animals.

Pets should not be allowed near food, dishes, worktops or food preparation areas.

Food safety and hygiene hints

- Do not leave perishable food at room temperatures for more than two hours. Perishable food brought from home, including sandwiches, should be kept in a fridge or cool place below 8°C.

- Insulated cool boxes, or a cool box with cool packs, should be used for carrying food when taking children on trips or outings.

- Eggs should be kept in the fridge.

- Eggs given to babies or toddlers should be cooked until both the yolk and the white are solid.

- Food stocks should be rotated and food beyond its use by date discarded.

- If food is to be eaten warm it should be re-heated until piping hot and then cooled down before serving.

- Avoid keeping food hot for long periods.

- Cool leftover food quickly and refrigerate.

- Do not use unpasteurised milk or milk-based products, such as cheese and yoghurt, made from unpasteurised milk. If a parent brings in goat's or sheep's milk for their child, check with the parent if the milk needs to be boiled.

- Root vegetables such as carrots and parsnips should always be peeled and topped and tailed. Fruit and vegetables to be eaten raw should be peeled for very young children, and washed well.

- Whole pieces of nut should not be given to under-5s in case of choking.

- Allergic reactions can be very serious. There should be a careful plan for choosing a safe and nutritious diet for any individual child with a true allergy.

General safety issues

- Children under 5 should never be left alone while they are eating, in case they choke.

- All highchairs should be fitted with a safety harness which should be used at all times when children are in the chairs. Children should never be left unsupervised while in a high chair.

For information on food safety and hygiene issues for infants, see page 39.

Bringing food from home

In some cases children may bring food from home to eat while they are in child care. It is helpful if the child care setting has its own nutrition policy (see example on page 52). This can be given to parents to help them in choosing and preparing food they send from home. It is reasonable to ask that children who bring food from home have similar food choices to the children who may have food provided for them in child care, particularly for snacks. A nutrition policy could request, for example, that children do not bring packets of crisps or confectionery with them. Discussions with parents are advised before changes are introduced.

Food for special occasions

Food is often eaten to celebrate special occasions. For example, sharing a birthday cake may be an important social activity.

Foods given as treats to mark special occasions are often based around sweet cakes and biscuits and there is nothing wrong with the occasional treat. Where a large number of children are cared for together, however, there may be so many birthdays and other special occasions (for example Christmas, Easter, Diwali, Eid-ul-Fitr, Halloween, Chinese New Year, or birth of new brothers and sisters) that it is almost a daily event. Carers may therefore wish to think of other special ways of celebrating. The children are also likely to celebrate outside of their child care so are unlikely to miss out on special foods. Decorating the room with balloons and streamers, encouraging children to dress up or wear party hats, playing party games and presenting foods in interesting shapes can make a party without the need for sweets, crisps, biscuits and cakes. A birthday cake made out of play dough with real candles will allow the ritual 'blowing out' of the candles to make the birthday child feel special.

Holidays, festivals and religious occasions of various cultures provide a valuable opportunity to include special occasion food and to involve the parents. The mix of children being cared for will determine which festivals in particular are celebrated, but it is important for children to learn and celebrate occasions and cultures not represented among them too. These events provide a springboard for all sorts of activities, not just those related to foods, and are an important part of the curriculum for children in school.

If parents wish to provide special treats for the children they could be encouraged to send in a variety of different foods. Let the parents know what policy you plan to take on special occasions and festivals so that they know what to send.

The box on the right shows a calendar of many of the main annual events.

Some of the most common festivals and celebrations throughout the year

January	1st: New Year
	6th: Epiphany: Three Kings Day
	7th: Rastafarian New Year
	25th: Burns' Night
Late January/ early February	Chinese New Year
	Jewish New Year for Trees
February	3rd: Japanese bean scattering
	14th: Valentine's Day
	40 days before Easter: Pancake Day (Shrove Tuesday)
Late February/ early March	Caribbean Carnival
	Chinese Festival of Light
	Purim (Jewish)
March	17th: St Patrick's Day
	Baha'i New Year
	Holi (Hindu Harvest Festival)
March/April	Mothering Sunday
	Passover (Jewish festival of Pesach)
	Easter
May	1st: May Day
	Wesak: Buddhist festival, first day of full moon in May
Late May/June	Shavuot: Jewish Festival of Weeks
	Tuan Yang Chieh: Chinese Dragon Boat Festival
August	Raksha Bhandhan: Indian celebration of brotherly/sisterly love
September/ early October	Jewish New Year: Yom Kippur
	Chinese Kite Festival
	Harvest Festival
October/ November	31st: Halloween
	Diwali: Hindu Festival of Light
November	5th: Guy Fawkes
	Thanksgiving
December	6th: St Nicholas
	Hanukkah (Jewish Festival)
	25th: Christmas Day
	26th: Boxing Day

Festivals such as Eid-ul-Fitr, the Islamic festival of fast breaking linked to Ramadan, occurs at a different time each year: parents will be able to advise carers on these dates. For a current calendar of religious festivals contact the SHAP Working Party (address on page 70).

Learning through food

Child care provides the opportunity for children to learn about food, food sources, nutrition, health, the seasons, growing cycles and other people's ways of life. Learning how to choose and enjoy many different nutritious foods in early childhood can provide the foundation for a lifetime of wise food choices.[13] Research suggests that even very young children are ready to learn more about food, nutrition and health than previously thought.[14, 15]

Activities involving food will encourage children both to develop a range of skills and also to increase their knowledge of food. They will also give children the opportunity to learn about new and different foods, and foods from a variety of cultures should be included (particularly those represented in the place of child care).

Carers can also involve children in preparing food and laying and clearing tables. This will all contribute to their educational experience.

> **Child care provides the opportunity for children to learn about food, food sources, nutrition, health, the seasons, growing cycles and other people's ways of life.**

Developing a nutrition policy

The best way to make sure that the recommendations and advice about healthy eating are agreed between the carer(s) and parents or guardians is to write a nutrition policy. This is not as difficult to do as it may sound: many child care settings already have a lot of 'unwritten' rules about food and eating. The advantage of writing them down as a 'policy' is that everyone has a chance to agree these ideas and in addition they provide information to new parents about your approach to healthy eating. This policy should not be seen as something set in stone, but something open to regular review.

A sample nutrition policy is given on the right as a guide to the sort of information that you may wish to include. Additional advice can be sought from State Registered Community Dietitians (for nurseries) or from local authorities (for childminders).

Food-related activities

• Making pictures with food - for example using dried pasta and pulses, rice, seeds or bay leaves

• Cutting out food pictures from magazines for collages, murals or mobiles

• Food prints: halved small potatoes, carrots, apples or parsnips

• Making a seed ball for the birds

• Papier maché fruit and vegetables

• Growing mustard and cress or sprouting seeds

• Making playdough or salt dough

• Having a pretend café or shop

• Food tasting

• Food smells game - for example spices, vinegar, orange, onion, strong cheese

• Food-related songs and rhymes - for example Five currant buns, Five little peas in a pea-pod pressed, Mix a pancake, Ten fat sausages.

Carers should positively encourage both boys and girls to participate in all activities, including food-related activities such as cooking.

Resources for encouraging learning through food-related activities can be found in Appendix 5.

Sample nutrition policy

• The weekly menu will be on display in advance. Recipes will be available to parents.

• The weekly menu will provide children in child care with a tasty, varied diet.

• All the children in child care will have suitable food made available for them.

• Children who do not receive breakfast at home will be offered this when they arrive if this is agreed with parents or guardians.

• Milk will be served with morning and afternoon snacks.

• All dairy products will be full fat.

• Soya drinks will only be given as a substitute for cow's milk with the parent's agreement and then only those fortified with calcium will be given.

• Water will be available at all times.

• Diluted fruit juice will be served with the main meal.

• Children will have access to bread or fruit if they are hungry between meals.

• Children will be allowed to have second helpings of fruit or milk-based desserts.

• Children will still receive dessert if they refuse their main course.

• Parents or guardians will be advised if their child is not eating well.

• Parents of children who are on special diets will be asked to provide as much information as possible about suitable foods and in some cases may be asked to provide the food themselves.

• Carers will sit with children while they eat and will provide a good role model for healthy eating.

• Withholding food will not be used as a form of punishment.

• Children will be encouraged to develop good eating skills and table manners and will be given plenty of time to eat.

• Advice will be given to parents about suitable foods to bring from home.

• Children will be encouraged to play outside every day, weather permitting. This will ensure that they have an opportunity to be exposed to summer sunlight which helps their bodies to make vitamin D.

Recommendations

Eating for health

- Children should be encouraged to eat a varied diet. They should eat foods from each of the four main food groups every day. The four main food groups are:
  - bread, other cereals and potatoes
  - fruit and vegetables
  - milk and dairy foods, and
  - meat, fish and alternatives such as pulses (peas, beans and lentils), and soya.

  A varied diet is associated with better health as it is more likely to contain all the nutrients the body needs.

- Fruit and vegetables are particularly important for good health. Under-5s should be encouraged to eat five child-sized portions of fruit and vegetables a day: for example, half an apple; two portions of vegetables (such as peas, carrots or tomatoes); a glass of fruit juice (diluted, and preferably served with a meal); and a small banana or a dried fruit snack (eg raisins).

- Vitamin C is important in maintaining good health and has a role in helping the body to absorb iron if both nutrients are present in the same meal. Under-5s should be encouraged to eat foods containing vitamin C - for example most fruit and fruit juices, potatoes, broccoli and other green vegetables, tomatoes and peppers. Eating five portions of fruit and vegetables a day (see recommendation above) will ensure an adequate vitamin C intake.

- It is recommended that children up to the age of 5 years should receive vitamin drops containing vitamins A, C and D. This is the responsibility of the parents or guardians but carers could provide information about where to find out more about them.

- The iron intake of children under 5 is lower than currently recommended and there is evidence to suggest that low iron status is common in this age group. Under-5s should therefore eat a diet that is high in iron-rich food such as meat, poultry and fish, as well as fruits and vegetables. (Meat and meat dishes are also a good source of zinc.) Children who do not eat meat should have a varied diet containing foods such as cereals, pulses (peas, beans and lentils), vegetables and fruits.

- The intakes of the type of sugars in the diet which most contribute to tooth decay are higher than recommended among the under-5s. If children have sugary foods, these should be given with meals rather than as snacks between meals. Children do not need sugary foods such as sweets, chocolate, soft drinks or honey for energy. Starchy foods - such as potatoes, bread, rice, pasta and yam - are better sources of energy as these foods contain other important nutrients too.

- It is important that the under-5s get enough energy (calories) for growth and development. While adults and children aged over 5 are encouraged to eat a diet that is high in starchy foods and low in fat, younger children on this sort of diet may not have the appetite to eat enough food to provide all the nutrients they need. Carers should therefore be sensitive to the needs of children who are fussy eaters or small eaters and ensure that these children are offered food that they will accept.

Drinks for 1 to 5 year olds

- Children should be encouraged to drink water if they are thirsty. Water quenches thirst, does not spoil the appetite, and does not damage teeth.

- Milk is a good drink for 1 to 5 year olds. Whole cow's milk is suitable as a main drink for most children from 12 months of age. Semi-skimmed milk can be introduced gradually after the age of 2 years, provided that the child is a good eater and has a varied diet. Skimmed milk is not suitable as the main drink for children under 5 years of age.

- Diluted fruit juice is a useful source of vitamin C. Children should be encouraged to have a glass of diluted fruit juice with their main meal or with breakfast as this may also help the body to absorb iron.

- Children should be discouraged from having fizzy drinks and squashes (including fruit squashes), both diet and non-diet, as these can erode the tooth enamel and contribute to tooth decay. Also, they provide little in the way of nutrients, and children who drink them frequently may have less appetite to eat well at mealtimes.

- If children are given soft drinks (such as squashes) containing the intense sweetener saccharin, these should be diluted more than they would be for an adult or older child - for example, 1 part squash to at least 8 parts water.

- Children who bring their own drinks to child care should be encouraged to bring a plastic flask or a lidded plastic cup containing an appropriately diluted drink. Many ready-to-drink cartons of squashes, fruit drinks and fruit juices have a high sugar content and cannot be diluted if they are drunk straight from the pack.

- Tea and coffee are not suitable drinks for under-5s as they contain tannic acid which interferes with iron absorption.

Dental health

- If children are having sugary foods and drinks, these should be given with meals rather than between meals. This is because children's first teeth are prone to decay if they are frequently in contact with sugars. It is important to reduce both the frequency and the total amount of sugar and sugary foods that children eat.

- To help the healthy development of teeth, children should not be given sweet drinks (such as fruit juice, squashes and other soft drinks) in a bottle or dinky feeder. A cup or beaker should be used if these drinks are given with meals.

- If a child uses a dummy or comforter, it should never be dipped into sugar or sugary drinks, as this can contribute to tooth decay.

- Some soft drinks which claim to have 'no added sugar' still contain sugars which are harmful to the teeth. Diet drinks, both fizzy and still, can also be harmful. This is because they may be acidic and erode the dental enamel, especially if sipped frequently. The use of these drinks should be avoided or limited.

Physical activity and outdoor play

- Children should be encouraged to be physically active and carers should timetable periods of activity into the children's daily routine throughout the year. Physical activity helps to ensure that children eat enough food and get all the nutrients they need. It also builds up muscle strength and overall fitness, develops physical skills such as balance and coordination, and provides a release for children's energy. Children who are physically active when they are young are more likely to maintain a healthy active lifestyle as they get older. This is important as an active lifestyle reduces the risk of ill health in adulthood.

- It is essential that there is outdoor space where children can play, or access to an outside area such as a garden, park or other safe open space. Exposure to summer sunlight in outdoor play helps children to maintain their vitamin D status. However, child care settings should have a 'sun policy', with guidelines on how long children can remain outdoors in strong sunshine, and on the use of protective clothing such as sunhats, and sunscreen. All under-5s should be appropriately supervised at all times while outdoors.

- Children in child care should have access to toys for active play - for example balls, hoops and skipping ropes.

Organisation of mealtimes and snacks

Timing of meals and snacks

- Breakfast is a particularly important meal and fortified breakfast cereals can make an important contribution to daily vitamin and mineral intakes. Parents and guardians should work together with carers to ensure that children have breakfast, either at home or in child care.

- Children need to eat regularly and it is recommended that children are offered something to eat at least every three hours.

- Children need nutritious snacks between meals. The best snacks are those which are low in added sugar. A variety of snacks should be offered including fruit, vegetables and any type of bread such as sandwiches, teacakes or fruit buns.

Creating the right atmosphere and encouraging social skills

- Meals can be times of pleasant social sharing. It is good practice for carers to sit with children during meals and snacks. It is important that what the carer eats and drinks provides a good role model for healthy eating.

- Mealtimes offer an opportunity to extend children's social and language skills. Children can learn from the carer about table manners, and can practise their speaking and listening skills. To encourage this, distractions such as television are best avoided during mealtimes.

- Children aged 2-5 years should be allowed to serve themselves during meals as this may encourage them to try different kinds of foods. Finger foods of all kinds, particularly fruit and vegetables, will encourage children under 2 years of age to feed themselves and try new foods. Child-sized utensils, crockery, tables and chairs may also make it easier for children to serve themselves and learn to eat independently.

- Children should be allowed to make their own food choices. If a child refuses a food or meal, the carer should gently encourage them to eat, but children should never be forced to eat. To minimise food refusal, it is important to ensure that a variety of foods are offered.

- Some children may eat slowly. It is important to ensure that all children have enough time to eat.

Involving parents and guardians

- A real partnership between parents or guardians and carers should be fostered. This could include:
  - making menus available to parents
  - giving parents adequate notice of any changes to meals, food choice or any other aspect of food provision, and allowing them to comment on and discuss the changes before they are introduced.

- Carers should give parents or guardians clear information each day about what food has been eaten and if their child has eaten well. Even older children may not be accurate in reporting what they have eaten.

- Carers should ask parents or guardians about any special dietary requirements their child has before the child starts attending the child care setting. Parents of children who are on special diets (for example a gluten-free diet), or who have food intolerances, are responsible for providing the carer with information about the food choices available to their child.

- Carers should seek advice from parents and guardians if they are serving food which the carers themselves are not familiar with. Such food should not only contain the right ingredients but should look and taste right too.

- Carers may wish to remind parents of the importance of giving vitamin drops to under-5s. Vitamin drops containing vitamins A, C and D are available free to families receiving Income Support or income-based Jobseeker's Allowance. Parents can get more information from their Health Visitor or GP.

Food hygiene and safety issues

- Carers should always wash their hands with soap and water before preparing food or helping children to eat, and after changing nappies and toileting children. If carers use a handkerchief while preparing food, they should wash their hands before continuing.

- Children's hands should always be washed with soap and water before meals and snacks, and after going to the toilet.

- Carers need to be aware of the requirements of the Food Safety Act. Some carers may need to complete a Food Hygiene Certificate course. Further information on this can be obtained from the local authority's environmental health department, or from its registration and inspection unit.

- Carers also need to be aware of food safety issues such as storage of food and leftover food, and thorough cooking or heating of foods. Several useful publications are available from the Ministry of Agriculture, Fisheries and Food (see Appendix 5). Carers should obtain and follow the advice in these. Some of the main points for carers are given in this chapter.

- Children under 5 should never be left alone while they are eating, in case they choke.

Learning through food

- Food can be used in a variety of educational ways, for example to teach children about food sources, nutrition, health, the seasons, growing cycles and other people's ways of life. Learning how to choose and enjoy many different nutritious foods in early childhood can provide the foundation for a lifetime of wise food choices.

- Carers should involve children in preparing food and laying and clearing tables.

- Holidays, festivals and religious occasions provide a valuable opportunity for children to learn about special events and different cultures and the variety of foods associated with these events.

Equal opportunities

- All children, and their parents or guardians, should be respected as individuals, and their food preferences and religious requirements should be accommodated.

- When planning food provision and menus, carers need to consider children who have special needs. Some children may have particular dietary requirements or may need specific help with eating, both of which are outside the scope of this report. Parents or guardians and carers may find it useful to contact support groups associated with the child's particular disability or need.

- Carers should positively encourage both boys and girls to participate in all activities, including food-related activities such as cooking.

- All that children bring with them to their place of child care - their race, gender, family background, language, culture and religion - should be valued in order for children to feel accepted and accepting of themselves. It is therefore important to value the contributions which different cultures and nationalities make to the variety of foods eaten in the UK today.

Chapter 6

Nutritional guidelines and menu planning

In this chapter the Expert Working Group makes recommendations for the amount of energy and nutrients that should typically be provided for a group of children aged under 5 who receive meals and snacks in child care or other early years settings.

Children have different needs depending on their age and gender, and the requirements of every child will be different. The recommendations therefore represent average intakes. If the food eaten by a group of children provides the amount of nutrients recommended, and the children receive the balance of their requirements at home, then the nutritional needs of most members of that group are likely to be met. The recommendations are not designed for individuals but act as a framework for menu planners and those advising menu planners on appropriate diets.

The recommendations have been set as percentages of the total daily intake of nutrients that an 'average' child requires. Children will spend different periods of time in child care and the recommendations consider the needs of children:

- in child care for a full day (8 hours or more)
- in half-day care which includes lunch, and
- in half-day care which includes tea (defined here as an afternoon meal).

These recommendations do not apply to children who attend playgroup, nursery units or reception classes for a period which does not include a meal. However, the general recommendations made in this report on nutritious snacks are relevant for these groups (see chapter 5).

'A table of food. Potatoes, a green apple, a red apple, Daddies sauce, plate of tomatoes, tomato ketchup, orange juice, fish on a plate.'

Robert, aged 4

Children in child care for a full day (8 hours or more)

Children in child care for a full day will receive the majority of their food while in child care and therefore it is recommended that the food provided gives the children at least 70% of their daily requirement for energy and nutrients. The remaining 30% will come from breakfast and from any drinks, snacks or light meals the child receives at home.

All children are encouraged to have breakfast. This could either be at home or in child care. Fortified breakfast cereals in particular provide a valuable source of some important vitamins and minerals. Parents and guardians and those providing child care should work together to ensure that children have breakfast either at home or in child care. The recommendations for daily intakes of nutrients do not include the contribution made by breakfast.

Nutritional guidelines for food prepared for children in full-day care are given in the box above. It is recommended that for these children there is provision for two meals (called here 'lunch' and 'tea') and two snacks (mid-morning snack and mid-afternoon snack). Food should be offered to children at intervals not exceeding three hours.

Two sample menus are shown on pages 59 and 60. These are given as a guide to the sorts of foods, quantities and distribution of food throughout the day which meet the nutritional guidelines and follow the healthy eating advice given elsewhere in this report.

The menus assume that children are drinking a third of a pint of whole cow's milk per day while in child care and that this is only part of their daily milk intake. Milk is an important part of the diet of children. Those children who do not drink milk will need to eat larger portions of food to make up the calories and other nutrients which would have been provided by milk. For children who do not want

Nutritional guidelines for food prepared for children in FULL-DAY CARE (8 hours or more)

Summary of recommendations

Energy	70% of the EAR
Protein	Not less than 70% of RNI
Fat	About 35% of food energy
Carbohydrate	About 50% of food energy
of which NME sugars	Not more than 10% of food energy
Thiamin	Not less than 70% of RNI
Riboflavin	Not less than 70% of RNI
Niacin	Not less than 70% of RNI
Vitamin C	Not less than 70% of RNI
Vitamin A	Not less than 70% of RNI
Iron	Not less than 80% of RNI
Calcium	Not less than 70% of RNI

Estimated Average Requirement (EAR)
The amount which satisfies 50% of the children in a group (defined by age and sometimes by gender).

Reference Nutrient Intake (RNI)
The amount of a nutrient which is sufficient to meet the dietary requirements for about 97% of the children in a group (defined by age and sometimes by gender). Intakes above this amount will almost certainly be adequate.

Percentage (%) of food energy
Percentage of calories consumed

to *drink* milk it can be included in the menu in custard, milk puddings, fromage frais, yoghurt and milk-based sauces. These foods should be encouraged for children who drink no milk for whatever reason. Advice on substitutes for milk drinks is given on page 44.

Fat

The current advice for adults and children over 5 years is to consume a diet in which about 35% of their daily energy needs are provided by the fat in food and added to food. The fat intake of children under 2 should not be restricted as the under-2s need foods which are energy-dense and nutrient-dense - that is, foods which pack a lot of calories and other nutrients into a small amount of food. It is important that children who have poor appetites or who are fussy

eaters get enough food that they will accept, to ensure their healthy growth and development. For more information about fat in the diet, see page 21.

Iron

The iron intake of children under 5 is lower than currently recommended and there is evidence to suggest that low iron status is common in this age group (see page 32). For this reason the Expert Working Group felt that the intakes of iron in the diet of children in child care should be enhanced to provide 80% of the recommended amount in full day care.

Iron will be particularly provided by main meals. Drinks (including milk) and many snacks are likely to be low in iron, so it is important that children receive the bulk of their iron from their meals. Good sources of iron are shown in

Appendix 1 and more information about iron in the diet and improving iron status is given on page 32.

Care needs to be taken when menu planning for children receiving a vegetarian diet to ensure they obtain sufficient iron. For more information about vegetarian diets, see page 49.

Worries about fatness in children

Parents or guardians who are concerned about their child being, or becoming fat, should encourage and enable the child to increase the amount of exercise he or she does each day. This can include activities done as part of the daily routine such as walking and climbing stairs, as well as physically active play such as running, ball games or playing in a playground. For more information about the importance of physical activity see page 20.

Children are unlikely to become fat if they eat, while in child care, the amount and types of food recommended in this book and if they follow the general advice it gives about healthy eating and physical activity. However, if they eat a significant amount of other foods as 'extras', particularly if these are high in calories but contain few other nutrients (for example sweets or soft drinks), then a child may take in more calories than they use up in their daily activities.

Restricting food intake among children (ie giving them less to eat than they would choose, or using 'low calorie' foods that are designed for adults) may prevent children from getting all the nutrients they need for normal growth and development. If parents or guardians have concerns about their child's weight they should ask their GP or Health Visitor for advice. The GP might refer the family to a State Registered Dietitian.

Children in half-day care

Half-day care involves either a morning or afternoon session and is likely to include one meal and at least one snack.

Breakfast is very important (see page 46) and children are encouraged to have breakfast either at home or in child care. Parents and guardians and those providing child care should work together to ensure that children have breakfast.

In order to set meaningful recommendations and to allow for the fact that lunch is likely to be the most substantial meal of the day, the nutritional guidelines for children in half-day care differ depending on whether lunch or tea is included in the child care schedule. 'Tea' in this context is defined as the afternoon 'meal', not as the afternoon snack.

Half-day care excluding a meal

Children in child care for a morning or afternoon period which does not include a meal should receive a snack during this period if the period of care exceeds two hours, and two snacks if this period is five hours or more but does not include a meal (for example 12.30pm - 5.30pm care, missing lunch and leaving before tea).

This report does not set specific guidelines for children who have only snacks and drinks while in child care. However, it is suggested that snacks and drinks offered are of similar nutritional value to those included in the menus outlined for children in longer periods of day care. They should also conform to the general guidelines given about snacks and drinks in this report (see pages 47 and 44).

Nutritional guidelines for food prepared for children in HALF-DAY CARE

Summary of recommendations

	Half-day including lunch and a snack	Half-day including tea* and a snack
Energy	40% of the EAR	30% of the EAR
Protein	Not less than 40% of RNI	Not less than 30% of RNI
Fat	About 35% of food energy	
Carbohydrate	About 50% of food energy	
of which NME sugars	Not more than 10% of food energy	
Thiamin	Not less than 40% of RNI	Not less than 30% of RNI
Riboflavin	Not less than 40% of RNI	Not less than 30% of RNI
Niacin	Not less than 40% of RNI	Not less than 30% of RNI
Vitamin C	Not less than 40% of RNI	Not less than 30% of RNI
Vitamin A	Not less than 40% of RNI	Not less than 30% of RNI
Iron	Not less than 45% of RNI	Not less than 35% of RNI
Calcium	Not less than 40% of RNI	Not less than 30% of RNI

* Tea is defined as the afternoon 'meal', not as the afternoon snack.

Estimated Average Requirement (EAR)
The amount which satisfies 50% of the children in a group (defined by age and sometimes by gender).

Reference Nutrient Intake (RNI)
The amount of a nutrient which is sufficient to meet the dietary requirements for about 97% of the children in a group (defined by age and sometimes by gender). Intakes above this amount will almost certainly be adequate.

Percentage (%) of food energy
Percentage of calories consumed

For information about the recommendations for fat and iron, see page 57.

Sample menus

Two sample menus are given on this page and page 60:

• Menu 1 is a sample menu for a one-week period. The foods and drinks in this menu provide the recommended amounts of energy and nutrients for children in child care for a full day. Children in half-day care including lunch would get the recommended amounts by having the mid-morning snacks and lunches shown on the menu. Children in half-day care including tea would get the recommended amounts by having the mid-afternoon snacks and teas.

• Menu 2 is a sample one-week menu which would be suitable for vegetarian children.

Menus 1 and 2 meet the nutritional guidelines for an average 3 year old in child care for a full day. A 4-5 year old will require, and want, larger portions at meals and snacks, as will children who do not drink milk. Water should always be available as a drink.

Menu 1 An example menu for a child in full day care

	Monday	Tuesday	Wednesday	Thursday	Friday
Example breakfast	Orange juice 25ml (diluted with water) cornflakes 15g milk 50ml brown toast 15g margarine 3g honey/jam 5g _Breakfast is encouraged either at home or in child care. This is not included in the nutritional analysis._				
Mid-morning snack eg at 10.00am	Milk 100ml muffin 40g margarine 4g	Milk 100ml crumpet 40g margarine 4g	Milk 100ml teacake 30g margarine 4g	Milk 100ml oatcake 26g margarine 4g	Milk 100ml scone 30g margarine 4g
Lunch eg 12.00-1.00 _Water offered as a drink_	Chicken and vegetable curry 100g rice 80g blackcurrant crumble 80g	Shepherd's pie 150g peas 30g stewed apple and dates 60g custard 60g	Tuna, bean and sweetcorn pasta 140g sponge pudding 60g custard 60g	Lamb burger 80g carrots 40g oven chips 50g rice pudding with sultanas 100g	Fish fingers 60g potatoes 60g broccoli 40g milk jelly 100g
Mid-afternoon snack eg at 3.00pm	Milk 100ml carrot sticks 30g brown bread 25g margarine 7g egg 25g	Milk 100ml apple 50g breadsticks 20g cheese 25g	Milk 100ml banana 50g plain popcorn 20g	Milk 100ml brown toast 25g margarine 7g marmite 2g raisins 20g	Milk 100ml flapjack 30g grapes 30g
Tea eg at 5.00pm	Orange juice 25ml (diluted with water) baked beans 80g brown toast 25g margarine 7g apple 50g fromage frais 60g	Orange juice 25ml (diluted with water) cheese 30g brown toast 25g margarine 7g celery 20g fruit salad 60g	Orange juice 25ml (diluted with water) scone 30g margarine 4g ham 20g cucumber 20g tinned pineapple 50g	Orange juice 25ml (diluted with water) pizza 60g tomato 40g apple 50g fruit yoghurt 60g	Orange juice 25ml (diluted with water) pasta 60g tomato sauce 40g cheese 20g mandarin orange 50g

Menu 2

This menu includes examples of meals, snacks and drinks which are suitable for vegetarian children and for particular ethnic groups. Individual menu planners will need to use their skill to provide meals that are acceptable to the particular group of children in their care.

	Monday	Tuesday	Wednesday	Thursday	Friday
Example breakfast	Orange juice 25ml (diluted with water) cornflakes 15g milk 50ml brown toast 15g margarine 3g honey/jam 5g *Breakfast is encouraged either at home or in child care. This is not included in the nutritional analysis.*				
Mid-morning snack eg at 10.00am	Milk 100ml muffin 40g margarine 4g	Milk 100ml crumpet 40g margarine 4g	Milk 100ml teacake 30g margarine 4g	Milk 100ml oatcake 26g margarine 4g	Milk 100ml scone 30g margarine 4g
Lunch eg 12.00-1.00 *Water offered as a drink*	Wholemeal cheese and egg quiche 100g baked beans 80g banana 50g	Fried tofu 60g stir-fried vegetables 80g noodles 60g milk/soya fruit yoghurt 60g	Potato curry 60g rice 80g dahl 50g chapati 20g orange 80g	Pasta 80g tomato sauce 40g cheese 20g broccoli 40g dried fruit salad 100g	Baked sweet potato 80g rice and peas 80g spinach 30g pineapple 80g
Mid-afternoon snack eg at 3.00pm	Milk 100ml carrot sticks 30g brown bread 25g margarine 7g egg 25g	Milk 100ml apple 50g breadsticks 20g cheese 25g	Milk 100ml banana 50g plain popcorn 20g	Milk 100ml brown toast 25g margarine 7g marmite 2g raisins 20g	Milk 100ml flapjack 30g grapes 30g
Tea eg at 5.00pm	Orange juice 25ml (diluted with water) cheese 30g brown toast 25g margarine 7g apple 50g fromage frais 60g	Orange juice 25ml (diluted with water) scrambled egg 60g brown toast 25g margarine 7g celery 20g fruit salad 60g	Orange juice 25ml (diluted with water) scone 30g hummus 15g cucumber 20g egg custard tart 60g	Orange juice 25ml (diluted with water) pizza 60g tomato 40g apple 50g fruit yoghurt 50g	Orange juice 25ml (diluted with water) pasta 60g cheese sauce 40g sweetcorn 30g mandarin orange 50g

Menu planning

Planning menus ahead will ensure that the best food choices are made and that meals are varied. When choosing meals to include in menus, remember that:

- A variety of foods should be served throughout the menu cycle.

- It is recommended that everyone includes more fruit and vegetables in their diet. Including fruit and vegetables at meals and as snacks will help to achieve this. Raw and cooked vegetables and fruit, diluted fruit juice and dried fruit all contribute to daily fruit and vegetable portions.

- Children need starchy foods for energy. These include bread, pasta, rice, potatoes, yam and sweet potato.

- Choose combinations of colours to make the food attractive. Three or four defined areas of colour look good on a plate.

- A combination of different textures increases appeal. Children will appreciate crisp, crunchy, chewy, smooth and soft foods.

- Taste should be varied but meals containing too many different or new flavours may not be acceptable to children.

- Some finger foods as well as foods which require cutlery allow variation at meal times.

Cost factors

Healthy eating need not be expensive. The amount of money available will have some influence on food choice but cost considerations should not be allowed to override the importance of providing a healthy and varied diet.

Some examples of ways to 'buy wisely' are given below.

- Offer pasta, rice and bread. All bread is a good source of nutrients. Some white breads and soft grain breads have extra nutrients added. Information will be given on the label.

- Use vegetables and fruit seasonally.

- If fresh fruit and vegetables are expensive or not available at certain times of year, use tinned or frozen ones.

- Meat will serve more people if you add vegetables, rice, pasta and pulses.

- Pulses, eggs and tinned fish are economical.

Spending money on cakes, biscuits, squashes and other soft drinks is poor nutritional value. These foods provide energy but few nutrients and may fill children up between meals with the result that they may not eat enough at mealtimes.

Recommendations

- The nutritional guidelines given on pages 57 and 58 should become standards for child care.

- Government departments should include reference to these nutritional guidelines in guidance and legislation on child care.

- Government and local authorities should include nutrition and nutritional guidelines in development plans for children under 5 in child care, and in plans for early years services and education.

- Local authorities should adopt the nutritional guidelines and use them as standards in the nurseries and child care settings which they contract, register, monitor and inspect.

- Local authorities should ensure that they either have, or have access to, appropriately skilled and trained staff to enable them to monitor nutritional standards in child care settings.

- Local authorities should provide the necessary training and information to enable individual carers to use the nutritional guidelines effectively.

- Registration and inspection officers should monitor the nutritional standards of the food served in the child care and other early years settings they visit. Inspectors' reports should include comments on food and nutrition. Appropriate expert advice and help should be offered to any child care or other early years setting which does not meet the guidelines.

- Registration and inspection officers should look for management commitment to nutritional training of a key person in each child care or other early years setting.

- Child care and other early years settings should be required, as part of the registration process, to demonstrate that they are committed to providing food which meets these guidelines.

- Nursery owners, managers, caterers, childminders and others responsible for early years services should seek appropriate information and training on how to meet the nutritional guidelines.

- NVQs, SVQs and the Certificate in Childcare and Education (CCE) are important training opportunities for carers and other early years staff. The information in this report should become an integral part of those qualifications within the relevant units. Other qualifications for those caring for under-5s should contain an appropriate section on nutrition and healthy eating.

- The European Commission should take account of the nutritional guidelines in this report when looking at European-wide nutritional standards for under-5s within the Community.

Appendix 1

Good sources of vitamins and minerals

This Appendix shows a number of foods and drinks which are important sources of certain vitamins and minerals. These are based on average servings.

	EXCELLENT	GOOD	USEFUL
B VITAMINS			
Thiamin	liver liver pâté pork, bacon, ham fortified breakfast cereal malted drinks	wholemeal bread yeast extract oatcakes currant buns ground up nuts potatoes	lean meat chicken and other poultry eggs white or brown bread semi-sweet biscuits
Riboflavin	liver kidney	milk malted drinks fortified breakfast cereal ground up almonds	lean meat or poultry bacon mackerel sardines tuna, salmon, pilchards cheese yoghurt eggs
Niacin	fortified breakfast cereals tuna canned salmon pilchards chicken	lean meat sausages kidneys herrings sardines	wholemeal bread peanut butter yeast extract bacon liver sausage
FOLATE	most fortified breakfast cereals, eg cornflakes, branflakes, crisped rice liver spinach	yeast extract cabbage spinach Brussels sprouts broccoli peas orange melon kidney	wholemeal bread/flour wheat bisks cauliflower beef runner beans tomatoes parsnip potatoes green leafy salads ackee ground up peanuts
VITAMIN C	blackcurrants orange (and juice) strawberries canned guava spring greens green and red peppers (raw)	broccoli cabbage cauliflower spinach tomato Brussels sprouts watercress kiwi fruit mango grapefruit	potatoes green beans peas satsumas eating apples nectarines peaches raspberries blackberries

	EXCELLENT	GOOD	USEFUL
VITAMIN A	liver liver sausage/pâté carrots spinach sweet potatoes watercress red peppers mango canteloupe melon dried apricots	nectarine peach blackcurrants fresh/canned apricots watercress tomatoes cabbage (dark) broccoli Brussels sprouts runner beans broad beans margarine butter cheese kidney	canned salmon herrings egg honeydew melon prunes orange sweetcorn peas whole milk
VITAMIN D	fortified breakfast cereals herrings pilchards sardines tuna canned salmon egg	liver (other than chicken liver) liver sausage/pâté margarine	chicken liver
CALCIUM	spinach sardines cheese tofu	pilchards yoghurt milk (whole/skimmed) soya drink fortified with calcium cheese spread	canned salmon muesli white bread/flour peas, beans and lentils dried fruit orange egg yolk
IRON	fortified breakfast cereals pig liver kidney chicken liver liver sausage/pâté	wholemeal bread/flour wheat bisks beef beefburger corned beef lamb sardines pilchards soya beans chick peas lentils spinach broccoli spring greens dried apricots raisins	white bread baked beans broad beans black-eyed peas blackcurrants salmon tuna herrings sausage chicken and other poultry egg tofu
ZINC	liver kidney lean meat corned beef	bacon ham poultry canned sardines shrimps and prawns tofu whole grain breakfast cereals, eg puffed wheat, branflakes, wheat bisks ground up nuts	sausages cold cooked meats canned tuna or pilchards eggs milk cheese beans and lentils brown or wholemeal bread plain popcorn sesame seeds and tahini

Appendix 2

Dietary Reference Values for energy and nutrients for under-5s

In 1991 the Department of Health Committee on Medical Aspects of Food and Nutrition Policy (COMA) published Dietary Reference Values which define the amounts of energy and nutrients that would meet the daily needs of most people in the UK.[1] The Dietary Reference Values include 'Estimated Average Requirements', and 'Reference Nutrient Intakes'. These terms are explained below.

Dietary Reference Values (DRVs)

Dietary Reference Values (DRVs) are benchmark intakes of energy and nutrients. They indicate the amount of energy or individual nutrients needed by a group of people of a certain age range (and sometimes gender) for good health. They are not designed for working out a diet for an individual; eating less of a nutrient than is recommended cannot tell us that an individual is deficient. However, if more than quite a few people in a group fall below the recommendations this suggests that some individuals in that population may be at risk of deficiency.

The DRVs for energy are described as the Estimated Average Requirement (EAR). Most other nutrients have an EAR and also a Reference Nutrient Intake (RNI) and a Lower Reference Nutrient Intake (LRNI). These terms are described below.

Estimated Average Requirement (EAR)

The average amount of energy or nutrients needed by a group of people. Half the population will have needs greater than this, and half will have needs below this amount.

Reference Nutrient Intake (RNI)

This is the amount of a nutrient which is enough to meet the dietary requirements of about 97% of a group of people. If people get more than this amount they will almost certainly be getting enough.

Lower Reference Nutrient Intake (LRNI)

This is the amount which is sufficient for the 3% of a group of people with the smallest needs. Most people will have needs greater than this.

Energy

The Estimated Average Requirements (EAR) for energy for children aged 6 months to 5 years - that is how many calories a day they need - are shown below.

Estimated Average Requirements for energy for children under 5 years

Age of child	Estimated Average Requirement in kcal (kJ) per day*	
	Boys	Girls
6 months	760 kcal (3,200 kJ)	710 kcal (2,980kJ)
9 months	880 kcal (3,680 kJ)	820 kcal (3,420kJ)
1 year	960 kcal (4,020 kJ)	910 kcal (3,800kJ)
1^1/2 years	1,080 kcal (4,520kJ)	1,020 kcal (4,260kJ)
2 years	1,190 kcal (4,960kJ)	1,130 kcal (4,720kJ)
2^1/2 years	1,280 kcal (5,370kJ)	1,230 kcal (5,140kJ)
3 years	1,490 kcal (6,230kJ)	1,370 kcal (5,730kJ)
4 years	1,600 kcal (6,730kJ)	1,460 kcal (6,120kJ)
5 years	1,720 kcal (7,190kJ)	1,550 kcal (6,480kJ)

* In practice the intakes of energy and of nutrients needs to be averaged over several days to take account of variations in appetite and in the diverse foods in a diet from day to day.

The energy we need every day is determined both by a basic level of requirement to keep our bodies functioning (called the Basal Metabolic Rate or BMR) and by the amount of physical activity that we do (for example moving around, walking, or exercising). People who are inactive have lower energy needs and will eat less food to maintain their body weight. It becomes much harder to get all the nutrients needed for good health if less food is eaten.

Protein

The Reference Nutrient Intakes for protein for infants and children under 5 years are summarised below.

	Reference Nutrient Intakes in grams per day
Infants 7-9 months	13.7
Infants 10-12 months	14.9
Children 1-3 years	14.5
Children 4-6 years	19.7

Fat and carbohydrate

There are no recommendations for the under-5s in terms of the proportion of energy in the diet which should come from fat and total carbohydrate. If under-5s have too little fat, this may affect their growth and development and their diet may be too low in other essential nutrients. Between the ages of 2 and 5 years children's diets should move towards the recommendations currently made for the over-5s. The recommendation currently made to restrict the amount of NME sugars in the diet to about 10% of energy intake is, however, appropriate for the under-5s.

Over the age of 5 years, the Dietary Reference Values for the intake of fat and carbohydrate expressed as the percentage of energy these contribute to the diet are that:

Total fat provides **no more than 35%** of energy

Saturated fats provide **no more than 11%** of energy

Total carbohydrate provides **50%** of energy

Intrinsic sugars, milk sugars and starch provide **at least 39%** of energy

Non-milk extrinsic sugars (NMES) provide **no more than 11%** of energy

The remaining 15% of energy will be contributed by protein.

Vitamins and minerals

The current Reference Nutrient Intakes for vitamins and minerals by infants and children under 5 years are summarised below.

Vitamins	7-9 months	10-12 months	1-3 years	4-6 years
Thiamin *mg/day*	0.2	0.3	0.5	0.7
Riboflavin *mg/day*	0.4	0.4	0.6	0.8
Niacin *mg/day*	4	5	8	11
Vitamin B6 *mg/day*	0.3	0.4	0.7	0.9
Vitamin B12 *ug/day*	0.4	0.4	0.5	0.8
Folate *ug/day*	50	50	70	100
Vitamin C *mg/day*	25	25	30	30
Vitamin A *ug/day*	350	350	400	500
Vitamin D *ug/day*	7	7	7	–*

Minerals	7-9 months	10-12 months	1-3 years	4-6 years
Calcium *mg/day*	525	525	350	450
Phosphorus *mg/day*	400	400	270	350
Magnesium *mg/day*	75	80	85	120
Potassium *mg/day*	700	700	800	1100
Iron *mg/day*	7.8	7.8	6.9	6.1
Zinc *mg/day*	5.0	5.0	5.0	6.5
Copper *mg/day*	0.3	0.3	0.4	0.6
Selenium *ug/day*	10	10	15	20
Iodine *ug/day*	60	60	70	100

* No Reference Nutrient Intake specified.

Appendix 3

Current intakes of energy and nutrients among the under-5s in Britain

This Appendix summarises the energy and nutrient intakes of children aged 1^1/$_2$ - 4^1/$_2$ years in Britain. The information is from *The National Diet and Nutrition Survey: Children Aged 1^1/$_2$ - 4^1/$_2$ Years.*[1] This study is the only recent, quantitative and representative survey of the eating patterns of young children available at the time of publication of this report.

Energy, protein, fat, carbohydrate and fibre intakes among children aged 1^1/$_2$ - 4^1/$_2$ years in Britain

	Boys/girls 1^1/$_2$ - 2^1/$_2$ yrs	Boys/girls 2^1/$_2$ - 3^1/$_2$ yrs	Boys 3^1/$_2$ - 4^1/$_2$ yrs	Girls 3^1/$_2$ - 4^1/$_2$ yrs	All
Total energy intake *kcal (MJ)/day*	1,045 (4.4)	1,160 (4.9)	1,273 (5.4)	1,183 (5.0)	1,141 (4.8)
Protein *g/day*	35.4	36.8	39.4	37.7	36.8
as % food energy	13.6	12.7	12.4	12.7	13.0
Fat *g/day*	42.5	46.3	50.1	47.2	45.7
as % food energy	36.4	35.8	35.3	35.5	35.9
of which saturated fatty acids *g/day*	19.7	20.8	21.9	20.6	20.6
as % energy	16.9	16.0	15.4	15.5	16.2
Starch, intrinsic sugars and milk sugars *g/day*	91	99	108	102	98
as % food energy	32.6	32.2	32.0	32.5	32.4
Non-milk extrinsic sugars (NME sugars) *g/day*	48	60	69	60	57
as % food energy	17.3	19.3	20.3	19.2	18.7
Fibre (Non-starch polysaccharides or NSP) *g/day*	5.5	6.2	6.8	6.4	6.1

Source: See reference 1.

Average intakes of vitamins from foods and supplements by children aged 1^1/$_2$ - 4^1/$_2$ years

	RNI		Average daily intake of children by age in years					% with intake less than RNI*	% with intake less than LRNI*
	1-3 yrs	4-6 yrs	1^1/$_2$-2^1/$_2$	2^1/$_2$-3^1/$_2$	Boys 3^1/$_2$-4^1/$_2$	Girls 3^1/$_2$-4^1/$_2$	All		
Vitamin A *ug/day*	400	400	589	579	568	561	578	44	8
Thiamin *mg/day*	0.5	0.7	0.8	0.8	0.9	0.9	0.8	10	<1
Riboflavin *mg/day*	0.6	0.8	1.2	1.2	1.2	1.2	1.2	6	<1
Niacin *mg/day*	8	11	14.9	16.4	18.2	17.5	16.3	0	0
Vitamin B6 *mg/day***	0.7	0.9	1.1	1.2	1.4	1.3	1.2	8	1
Folate *ug/day*	70	100	120	134	145	140	132	6	<1
Vitamin C *mg/day*	30	30	50.7	52.2	54.6	50.0	51.8	38	1
Vitamin D *ug/day*	7	–	1.8	1.8	2.0	1.9	1.9	n/a***	n/a

*   The percentage of children with reported intakes below the RNI and LRNI are given for children aged 4 years and under only.

**   Vitamin B6 requirements are based on protein providing 14.7% of the Estimated Average Requirement for food energy.

*** Vitamin D is found in some foods and is also made in the skin following exposure to summer sunlight. Dietary intake of vitamin D alone does not provide useful information about the proportion of this population who may be at risk of low vitamin D status.

Source: See reference 1.

Average intakes of minerals from foods and supplements by children aged 1¹/₂ - 4¹/₂ years

	RNI		Average daily intake of children by age in years					% with intake less than RNI*	% with intake less than LRNI*
	1-3 yrs	4-6 yrs	1¹/₂-2¹/₂	2¹/₂-3¹/₂	Boys 3¹/₂-4¹/₂	Girls 3¹/₂-4¹/₂	All		
Iron *mg/day*	6.9	6.1	5.0	5.6	6.2	5.9	5.5	84	16
Calcium *mg/day*	350	450	663	635	625	595	637	11	1
Phosphorus *mg/day*	270	350	735	740	767	736	742	1	n/a
Magnesium *mg/day*	85	120	132	137	146	137	136	7	<1
Potassium *mg/day*	800	1100	1,476	1,513	1,573	1,501	1,508	3	<1
Zinc *mg/day*	5.0	6.5	4.3	4.4	4.7	4.4	4.4	72	14
Copper *mg/day*	0.4	0.6	0.4	0.5	0.5	0.5	0.5	36	n/a
Iodine *ug/day*	70	100	123	117	121	113	119	24	3

* The percentage of children with reported intakes below the RNI and LRNI are given for those aged 4 years and under only.

Source: See reference 1.

Percentage of 1¹/₂ - 4 year old children in Britain with intakes of iron, zinc, vitamin A and vitamin C below the Reference Nutrient Intake

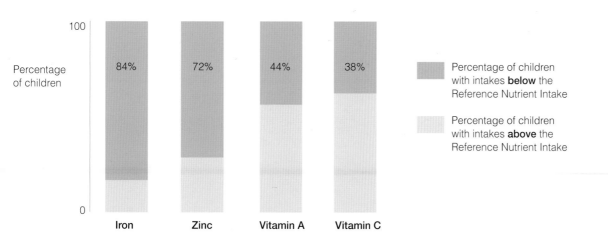

Source: See reference 1.

Appendix 4

Food-related customs

This is a guide to some of the differences in food choice commonly observed by those from different religious and cultural groups. It is important to emphasise that there may be individual differences in food choices between families, and those providing child care should not make assumptions about anyone's food preferences. It is important to find out about each child from his or her parent or guardian.

'Some' means that some people within a religious group would find these foods acceptable.

	Jewish	Hindu[1]	Sikh[1]	Muslim	Buddhist	Rastafarian[2]
Eggs	No blood spots	Some	Yes	Yes	Some	Some
Milk/yoghurt	Not with meat	Yes	Yes	Yes	Yes	Some
Cheese	Not with meat	Some	Some	Possibly	Yes	Some
Chicken	Kosher	Some	Some	Halal	No	Some
Mutton/lamb	Kosher	Some	Yes	Halal	No	Some
Beef and beef products	Kosher	No	No	Halal	No	Some
Pork and pork products	No	No	Rarely	No	No	No
Fish	With fins and scales	With fins and scales	Some	Some	Some	Yes
Shellfish	No	Some	Some	Some	No	No
Butter/ghee	Kosher	Some	Some	Some	No	Some
Lard	No	No	No	No	No	No
Cereal foods	Yes	Yes	Yes	Yes	Yes	Yes
Nuts/pulses	Yes	Yes	Yes	Yes	Yes	Yes
Fruits/vegetables	Yes	Yes[3]	Yes	Yes	Yes	Yes
Fasting[4]	Yes	Yes	Yes	Yes	Yes	Yes

1 Strict Hindus and Sikhs will not eat eggs, meat, fish, and some fats.

2 Some Rastafarians are vegan.

3 Jains have restrictions on some vegetable foods. Check with the individuals.

4 Fasting is unlikely to apply to young children.

Appendix 5

Useful addresses and further information

Useful addresses

Association of Breastfeeding Mothers
PO Box 441
St Albans
Herts AL4 0AS
Tel: 01171-813 1481

British Allergy Foundation
Deepdene House
30 Bellegrove Road
Welling
Kent DA16 3BY
Tel: 0181-303 8525

British Dental Association
64 Wimpole Street
London W1N 8AL
Tel: 0171-935 0875

British Dietetic Association (Paediatric Group)
7th Floor
Elizabeth House
22 Suffolk Street
Queensway
Birmingham B1 1LS
Tel: 0121-643 5483

Chartered Institute of Environmental Health
Chadwick Court
15 Hatfields
London SE1 8DJ
Tel: 0171-928 6006

Community Practitioners' and Health Visitors' Association (CPHVA)
50 Southwark Street
London SE1 1UN
Tel: 0171-717 4000

Daycare Trust
4 Wild Court
London WC2B 4AU
Tel: 0171-405 5617

Health Education Authority
Trevelyan House
30 Great Peter Street
London SW1P 2HW
Tel: 0171-222 5300

Health Education Authority publications are available either from your local Health Promotion Unit, or from:
Health Education Authority
Customer Services
Marston Book Services
PO Box 269
Abingdon
Oxon OX14 4YN
Tel: 01235-465565
See also *Health Education Authority publications* on page 70.

Health Education Board for Scotland
Woodburn House
Canaan Lane
Edinburgh EH10 4SG
Tel: 0131-536 5500

Kids' Club Network
Bellerive House
3 Muirfield Crescent
London E14 9SZ
Tel: 0171-512 2112

La Leche League
BM 3424
London WC1N 3XX
Tel: 0171-242 1278

Maternity Alliance
45 Beech Street
London EC2P 2LX
Tel: 0171-588 8582

National Asthma Campaign
Providence House
Providence Place
London N1 0NT
Tel: 0171-226 2260

National Childbirth Trust
Alexandra House
Oldham Terrace
London W3 6NH
Tel: 0181-992 8637

National Childminding Association
8 Masons Hill
Bromley
Kent BR2 9EY
Tel: 0181-464 6164

National Children's Bureau
Early Childhood Unit
8 Wakley Street
London EC1V 7QE
Tel: 0171-843 6000

National Council of Voluntary Child Care Organisations
Unit 4
Pride Court
80-82 White Lion Street
London N1 9PF
Tel: 0171-833 3310

National Private Day Nurseries Association
Gothic House
Barker Gate
Nottingham NG1 1JU
Tel: 0115-912 3401

Northern Ireland Pre-school Playgroup Association (NIPPA)
Enterprise House
Boucher Crescent
Boucher Road
Belfast BT12 6HU
Tel: 01232-662825

Parents at Work
45 Beech Street
London EC2Y 8AD
Tel: 0171-628 3565

Pre-school Learning Alliance
69 Kings Cross Road
London WC1X 9LL
Tel: 0171-833 0991

Royal Institute of Public Health and Hygiene and the Society of Public Health
28 Portland Place
London W1N 4DE
Tel: 0171-580 2731

Scottish Pre-school Play Association
14 Elliot Place
Glasgow G3 8EP
Tel: 0141-221 4148/9

Vegan Society
Donald Watson House
7 Battle Road
St Leonard's on Sea
East Sussex TN37 7AA
Tel: 01424-427393

Vegetarian Society
Parkdale
Dunham Road
Altrincham
Cheshire WA14 4QG
Tel: 0161-928 0793

Wales Pre-school Playgroups Association
2a Chester Street
Wrexham LL13 8BD
Tel: 01978-358195

Working for Childcare
77 Holloway Road
London N7 8JZ
Tel: 0171-700 0281

Further reading

Child Development from Birth to Eight: A Practical Focus
National Children's Bureau, London.
ISBN 1 874579 09 1

Young Children in Group Day Care: Guidelines for Good Practice
National Children's Bureau, London.
ISBN 1 874579 40 7

Oral Health Strategy for Scotland
Available from the Health Education Board for Scotland (address on the left).

Department of Health publications

Available from:
Department of Health
PO Box 410
Wetherby LS23 7LN
Tel: 01937-840250
Fax: 0990-210266

Breast Feeding: Good Practice Guidance to the NHS. Booklet

What's for Dinner Today Mum? A Short Guide to Weaning. Leaflet and poster

Practical Food Hygiene. Poster

Welfare Milk and Vitamins: A Guide for Families. Leaflet

Health Education Authority publications

Available from:
HEA Customer Services
Marston Book Services
PO Box 269
Abingdon
Oxon OX14 4YN
Tel: 01235-465565

Some publications are priced but may be available free from your local Health Promotion Unit (in the phone book under the name of your local health authority). If you live in Scotland contact your local health board or the Health Education Board for Scotland for these or similar publications (address on page 69).

Birth to Five
Book. ISBN 0 752108 95 6. A complete guide to the first five years of being a parent. Available free to all first time parents through Health Promotion Units.

Breastfeeding Your Baby
Leaflet. ISBN 0 752108 71 9

Weaning Your Baby
Leaflet. ISBN 0 752108 72 7

Keeping Baby Teeth Healthy: Tooth Care for 0-2 Year Olds
Booklet.
ISBN 0 752107 15 1

Caring for Your Children's Teeth: Tooth Care for 3-11 Year Olds
Booklet.
ISBN 0 752107 16 X

If You Worship the Sun Don't Sacrifice Your Skin: How to Protect Your Skin From Sun Damage
Booklet.
ISBN 0 752107 00 3

Ministry of Agriculture, Fisheries and Food publications

Available free from:
Foodsense
Admail 6000
London SW1A 2XX
Tel: 0645-556000

Healthy Eating for Infants and Young Children
PB3036

Healthy Eating PB0550

Understanding Food Labels PB0553

Use Your Label: Making Sense of Nutrition Information PB2362

About Food Additives PB0552

Food Safety PB0551

Keeping Food Cool and Safe PB1649

Food Allergy and Other Unpleasant Reactions to Food PB1696

Ten Tips for Food Safety PB1684: posters in A5, A4 or A2 sizes

The Food Safety Act 1990 and You
Booklet summarising the Food Safety Act. PB2507

Be Allergy Aware
Advice for catering establishments. Booklet PB3318. Poster PB3317

Food Hygiene with Hy-Genie!
Pack including posters, wallchart and stickers. PB0305.
Accompanying video available from CFL Vision, PO Box 35, Wetherby, Yorks LS23 7EX. Price £8.50 plus VAT.

Cookery books

Baby and Toddler Cookbook
Annabel Karmel
Ebury Press, London
ISBN 0 09 178354 2

Baby and Toddler Meal Planner
Annabel Karmel
Ebury Press, London
ISBN 0 09 186360 0

First Food Made Fun
Miriam Stoppard
Dorling Kindersley Ltd, London
ISBN 07513 0007 1

The Nursery Food Book
Mary Whiting and Tim Lobstein
Arnold (Hodder Headline), London
ISBN 0 340 71894 3

Small Helpings
Annabel Karmel
Ebury Press, London
ISBN 0 09 186373 2

Books on festivals and celebrations

Celebration!
Barnabas and Annabel Kindersley
Dorling Kindersley Ltd, London
ISBN 0 7513 5650 6

Festival Booklets Set
NES Arnold (address on page 71).
NB3888/1

Festivals and Celebrations
Jim Fitzsimmons and Rhona Whiteford
Scholastic Educational Books (address on page 71)
ISBN 0 590 53083 6

'SHAP' calendar of religious festivals
A calendar of festivals for the current year. Available from:
SHAP Working Party
c/o National Society Religious Education Centre
36 Causton Street
London SW1P 4AU
Tel: 0171-932 1194

Books on learning through play

Clay and Dough
Lynne Burgess
Scholastic Educational Books (address on page 71).
ISBN 0 590 53638 9

Food
Lesley Clark
In the 'Themes for Early Years' series.
Scholastic Educational Books (address on page 71).
ISBN 0 590 53719 9

Food Glorious Food
A tape of songs for ages 3 and over.
Early Learning Centre (address on page 71).
Ref 37556

Multi-cultural Play
NES Arnold (address on page 71).
NB3370/5

Sources of resource material for food-related activities

Catalogues are available from the following companies.

ASCO Educational Supplies Ltd
19 Lockwood Way
Parkside Lane
Leeds LS11 5TH
Tel: 0113-270 7070

Early Learning Centre
South Marston Park
Swindon SN3 4TJ
Tel: 01793-831300

The Festival Shop Ltd
56 Poplar Road
Kings Heath
Birmingham B14 7AG
Tel: 0121-444 0444
Can provide a small catalogue which includes a calendar of cultural events.

Galt Educational
Culvert Street
Oldham
Lancashire OL4 2ST
Tel: 0161-627 0795

Hope Education
Orb Mill
Huddersfield Road
Waterhead
Oldham
Lancashire OL4 2ST
Tel: 0161-633 6611

NES Arnold
Ludlow Hill Road
West Bridgeford
Nottingham NG2 1BR
Tel: 0115-945 2201

Pictorial Charts Educational Trust
27 Kirchen Road
London W13 OUD
Tel: 0181-567 5343

Schofield and Sims Ltd
Dogley Mill
Fenay Bridge
Huddersfield
West Yorkshire
HD8 0NQ
Tel: 01484-607080
Fruit and vegetable wall charts.

Scholastic Educational Books
FREEPOST CV 3067
Leamington Spa
Warwickshire
CV33 0BR
Tel: 01926-887799

CHAPTER 1

1 Gregory JR, Collins DL, Davies PSW, Hughes JM, Clarke PC. 1995. *National Diet and Nutrition Survey: Children Aged 1^{1}/2 to 4^{1}/2 Years. Volume 1. Report of the Diet and Nutrition Survey.* London: HMSO.

2 Department of Health. 1998. *Children's Day Care Facilities at 31 March 1997. England.* (A/F 97/6.)

CHAPTER 2

1 Gregory JR, Collins DL, Davies PSW, Hughes JM, Clarke PC. 1995. *National Diet and Nutrition Survey: Children Aged 1^{1}/2 to 4^{1}/2 Years. Volume 1. Report of the Diet and Nutrition Survey.* London: HMSO.

2 Department of Health. 1998. *Children's Day Care Facilities at 31 March 1997. England.* (A/F 97/6.)

3 Dewey C, Golding J. 1996. *Descriptive Observations of Day Care Used in the First 18 Months by the ALSPAC Children in Focus Sample.* Bristol: University of Bristol.

4 Pupils under 5 years in each Local Education Authority, England - January 1996. *Statistical Bulletin 2/97.* London: Department for Education and Employment.

5 Working for Childcare. 1995. *Survey of Employer Supported Day Nurseries in England and Wales.* London: Working for Childcare.

6 Srivastava A. 1996. *The Nutritional Intake of 16 Children at a Day Nursery in the London Borough of Hounslow.* London: University of North London.

7 Rowley C. 1996. *A Comparison of the Nutritional Quality and Contribution of Midday Meals to Diets of Pre-school Children Attending a Private, Council and Community Nursery in an Inner London Borough.* London: University of North London.

CHAPTER 3

1 Department of Health. 1991. *Dietary Reference Values for Food Energy and Nutrients for the United Kingdom. Report on Health and Social Subjects No. 41.* London: HMSO.

2 Gregory JR, Collins DL, Davies PSW, Hughes JM, Clarke PC. 1995. *National Diet and Nutrition Survey: Children Aged 1^{1}/2 to 4^{1}/2 Years. Volume 1. Report of the Diet and Nutrition Survey.* London: HMSO.

3 Dietz WH, Gortmaker SL. 1985. Do we fatten our children at the TV set? Television viewing and obesity in children and adolescents. *Paediatrics*; 75: 807-812.

4 Fontveille AM, Harper IT, Ferraro T, Spraul M, Ravussin E. 1993. Daily energy expenditure by five year old children measured by doubly labelled water. *Journal of Paediatrics;* 123: 201-206.

5 Goran MI, Carpenter WH, Poehlman ET. 1993. Total energy expenditure in 4 to 6 year old children. *Americal Journal of Physiology*; 264: E706-E711.

6 Wallace W. 1996. Food for thought. *Nursery World*; 96: 8-9.

7 Prentice A, Jebb S. 1995. Obesity in Britain: Gluttony or sloth? *British Medical Journal*; 311: 437-439.

8 Health Education Authority. 1997. *Young and Active? Draft Policy Framework for Young People and Health-enhancing Physical Activity.* London: Health Education Authority.

9 Department of Health. 1994. *Weaning and the Weaning Diet. Report on Health and Social Subjects No. 45.* London: HMSO.

10 World Health Organization. 1984. *Prevention Methods and Programmes for Oral Diseases. WHO Technical Report Series No. 713.* Geneva: World Health Organization.

11 Department of Health. 1989. *Dietary Sugars and Human Disease. Report of the Committee on Medical Aspects of Food Policy.* London: HMSO.

12 Health Education Authority. 1990. *Sugars in the Diet: Briefing Paper.* London: Health Education Authority.

13 Hinds K, Gregory J. 1995. *National Diet and Nutrition Survey: Children Aged 1^1/2 - 4^1/2 Years. Volume 2: Report of the Dental Survey.* London: HMSO.

14 Holt RD. Winter GB, Downer MC, Bellis MJ, Hay IS. 1996. Caries in pre-school children in Camden 1993/94. *British Dental Journal*; 181: 405-411.

15 Health Education Authority. 1996. *How to Protect Your Skin From Sun Damage.* London: Health Education Authority.

16 Duggan MB. 1992. The weaning diet of healthy Asian children living in Sheffield. 1. The level and composition of the diet in children from 4-40 months of age. *Journal of Human Nutrition and Dietetics*; 5: 189-200.

17 James J, Evans J, Male P, Pallister C, Hendrikz JK, Oakhill A. 1988. Iron deficiency in inner city pre-school children: development of a general practice screening programme in an inner city practice. *Journal of the Royal College of General Practitioners*; 38: 250-252.

18 Dallman PR, Simes MA, Stekel A. 1980. Iron deficiency in infancy and childhood. *American Journal of Clinical Nutrition;* 33: 86-118.

19 Harris RJ, Armstrong D, Ali R, Loynes A. 1983. Nutritional survey of Bangladeshi children under 5 years in the London Borough of Tower Hamlets. *Archives of Diseases of Childhood;* 58: 428-432.

20 Williams S, Sahota P. 1990. An enquiry into the attitudes of Muslim Asian mothers regarding infant feeding practices and dental health. *Journal of Human Nutrition and Dietetics*; 3: 393-402.

21 Fuchs GJ, Farris RP, De Weir M. 1993. Iron status and intake of older infants fed formula versus cow's milk with cereal. *American Journal of Clinical Nutrition*; 58: 343-348.

22 Ministry of Agriculture, Fisheries and Food. 1997. *Healthy Diets for Infants and Young Children.* London: Ministry of Agriculture, Fisheries and Food in association with the Department of Health and the Health Education Authority. Available from Foodsense, London SE99 7TT.

CHAPTER 4

1 Puczynski M, Rademaker D, Gatson R. 1983. Burn injury related to the improper use of a microwave oven. *Paediatrics*: 72: 5.

2 Department of Health. 1998. *Report on Peanut Allergy. Committee on Toxicity of Chemicals in Food, Consumer Products and the Environment (COT).* London: The Stationery Office.

CHAPTER 5

1 Dowler E, Calvert C. 1995. *Nutrition and Diet in Lone-parent Families in London.* London: Family Policy Studies Centre.

2 Kant AK, Schatzkin A, Harris TB, Ziegler RG, Block G. 1993. Dietary diversity and subsequent mortality in the First National Health and Nutrition Examination Survey Epidemiological Follow-Up Study. *American Journal of Clinical Nutrition*; 57: 434-440.

3 Story M, Brown JE. 1987. Do young children instinctively know what to eat? The studies of Clara David revisited. *New England Journal of Medicine;* 316: 103-106.

4 Rolls BJ. 1985. Experimental analyses of variety in a meal on human feeding. *American Journal of Clinical Nutrition;* 42: 932-939.

5 Health Education Authority. 1995. *Enjoy Healthy Eating.* London: Health Education Authority.

6 Birch LL, McPhee L, Shoba BC, Pirok E, Steinberg L. 1987. What kind of exposure reduces children's food neophobia? *Appetite*; 9: 171-178.

7 Nahikan-Nelms M. 1997. Influential factors of caregiver behaviour at mealtime: a study of 24 child-care programs. *Journal of the American Dietetic Association;* 97: 505-509.

8 Gregory JR, Collins DL, Davies PSW, Hughes JM, Clarke PC. 1995. *National Diet and Nutrition Survey: Children Aged 1^1/2 to 4^1/2 Years. Volume 1. Report of the Diet and Nutrition Survey.* London: HMSO

9 Health Education Authority. 1997. *Young and Active? Draft Policy Framework for Young People and Health-enhancing Physical Activity.* London: Health Education Authority

10 Hourihane JO'B, Rolls CJ. 1995. Morbidity from excessive intake of high energy fluids: the 'squash drinking syndrome'. *Archives of Diseases of Childhood;* 72: 141-143.

11 Hinds K, Gregory J. 1995. *National Diet and Nutrition Survey: Children Aged 1^1/2 - 4^1/2 Years. Volume 2: Report of the Dental Survey.* London: HMSO.

12 Department of Health. 1998. *Report on Peanut Allergy. Committee on Toxicity of Chemicals in Food, Consumer Products and the Environment (COT).* London: The Stationery Office.

13 Farthing MAC, Phillips MG. 1987. Nutrition standards in day-care programs for children. *Journal of the American Dietetic Association*; 87: 503-506.

14 Singleton JC, Achterburg CL, Shannon B. 1992. The role of food and nutrition in the health perceptions of young children. *Journal of the American Dietetic Association;* 92: 67-70.

15 Anliker JA, Laus MJ, Sammonds KW, Beal VA. 1990. Parental messages and the nutrition awareness of preschool children. *Journal of Nutrition Education*; 22: 24-29.

APPENDIX 2

1 Department of Health. 1991. *Dietary Reference Values for Food Energy and Nutrients for the United Kingdom. Report on Health and Social Subjects No. 41.* London: HMSO.

APPENDIX 3

1 Gregory JR, Collins DL, Davies PSW, Hughes JM, Clarke PC. 1995. *National Diet and Nutrition Survey: Children Aged 1^1/2 to 4^1/2 Years. Volume 1: Report of the Diet and Nutrition Survey.* London: HMSO.